A Pilgrimage on the Camino de Santiago

2013

Terry McHugh

Contents

Acknowledgements

Many thanks to the organisations that have made much of the history available on their web sites

Irish Society of the Friends of St.James (Cumann Cáirde San Séamus i nÉirinn)

The Confraternity of Saint James (British)

New Advent

Via Compostela

And the help given to me for my pilgrimage by the many great people on the Camino de Santiago forum

ISBN: 1500997242

ISBN-13: 978-1500997243

Dedications

This book is dedicated to my long suffering wife, Margaret and our family who have been extremely supportive of my absences from home to walk 'El Camino' and have remained supportive when I announced that I am going back in 2015.

Also to the many friends I met along the way and in particular;

Mees van der Sluijs, from the Netherlands without whose help I doubt I would have ever made it to Santiago

Lynne from New Zealand who guided me down the mountain at El Acebo

And Nicole from the Netherlands who helped me through an evening when I was sick and dehydrated also in El Acebo

Muchas Gracias mi Amigos

Foreword

In 2013, I chose to complete my 'way' after my son had completed his in 2012 and had urged me to do the same. What follows is my story, slightly different from other Camino stories. While others start from St Jean Pied de Port and finish when they walk into Santiago, my story begins in Pamplona, but unlike other peregrinos who have recounted their pilgrimage, mine stops in Castrojeriz when I give up too easily and go home only to find the determination to go back and complete it just five months later.

When I arrived home from Santiago and began the task of committing my journal to digital format, I realised that although I had walked the Camino, I really knew nothing about it, or for that matter, Spain. As my curiosity grew I started to research it and I became completely immersed in the project so much so that I realised that digitising my journal had turned into the foundations of a book.

I hope you find the history informative and the daily record of my pilgrimage interesting but if not maybe it will help you overcome insomnia. If it inspires just one to pull on their boots and head for Santiago, then it has been a worthwhile project. If the Camino calls, answer it. Don't make excuses about age or health. I met a woman in her eighties skipping along and another in the twilight of her life hobbling along on walking sticks, crippled with arthritis and she had walked further than I had. You will find it very rewarding, if not spiritually, then in your waist size. Don't ignore the call, follow it and experience emotions you did not know you had.

Walk With The Sun
Till Your Shadow
Disappears

My Camino 2013

By Terry McHugh

Introduction

In the spring of 2012, I began planning my Camino. Why? I don't really know. I won't bore you with reasons of spirituality, getting closer to God or sorting my life out. Maybe those are the reasons of other pilgrims, but for me? I am not the spiritual kind, I am a Sunday Catholic and quite frankly, my life is pretty good. There are many worse off than me. Maybe I will figure it out later but for now my only reason is to 'just do it'.

When my son Christopher was made redundant in January of 2012, he saw it as an opportunity to walk his Camino and he had asked me to go with him. I turned him down because; let's face it, who had ever heard of a man of my age walking 500 miles? I had retired three years previously after 35 years sitting on my backside in an office, getting fat and growing more unfit by the day. I had a cruise booked for May and was afraid that I might be injured in some way and not be able to go on it, besides, I didn't really think Chris would go. When he announced he had his flights and trains booked I was taken aback and secretly hoped he would not go as I felt he was putting himself in danger, after all, until a few short weeks ago, I had never heard of El Camino de Santiago. But on my 63rd birthday, February 28th, he set off for London then on to France. Without going into the details of his Camino, I started to regret not going with him as I tracked his progress day by day on maps and Google Earth. The idea was now taking hold in my mind that I would do it next year and I started walking around the local park to try to get some level of fitness and eventually I set my plans for Easter 2013. By Halloween, I had flights booked for both of us as Chris had agreed to come with me for the first two weeks. By Christmas I had purchased most of the gear I was going to need, plus some, and it was just a case of waiting for the day of departure, the 16th March.

The 13th March came and with it, our first hurdle. It had all seemed so simple when I started planning this last spring. Fly to London then on to Biarritz which at the time appeared to be the most difficult thing to arrange. After that the train to St Jean Pied de Port was easy. Arrive in town on the 16th March and start walking on St Patrick's Day. Easy Peasy, or was it?

The weather has, over the course of history, changed the plans of many adventurers and now the unpredictable nature of it threw my plans into disarray. The Pyrenees, in fact the whole of northern Spain, was experiencing the worst winter and spring weather in twenty years. Route Napoleon was, as is usual in March, closed, but this year it would probably remain closed until well into May. Snow drifts were reaching 6 to 9 feet and even the trails along the Val Carlos valley were closed. The only way to Roncesvalles was by road slogging which in itself can be dangerous in poor visibility. To hell with that I thought, it was a pilgrimage we were going on, not a death defying adventure competing for space on icy roads with cars and trucks. It's one thing risking my own life, but I couldn't ask my son to risk his. The trouble was, I didn't have a plan B so I had to formulate one in a hurry. After a bit of research I found an evening bus from Biarritz to Pamplona so that was plan B I reckoned. That was easy. Why does everyone worry about how to get to the other side of the mountains?

I don't know why I double checked but it would not be the only time I would do this over the following few weeks thus averting a right royal cock up. The bus doesn't run during March so it was back to the drawing board. Margaret's old story about boats and helicopters was coming to mind. Was someone or something telling me not to go? I didn't buy into that old story, it was just life throwing me some hurdles to overcome and sure, without challenges life would be one long bore.

Well, this was my solution. From Biarritz airport we could get a bus to the train station, then a train to Hendaye on the French/Spanish border. Catch the Euskotren to Donostia/San Sebastian, and catch the bus from there to Pamplona and check in to the Hostel Hemingway. It all sounded easy but there was still a slight problem. We had only twenty minutes to get from the Euskotren stop to the bus station in Donostia/San

Sebastian. Could we do it? Half a mile with rucksacks on, buy tickets and find the bus. We would find out soon enough. They say no-one does the Camino without help. I hadn't even left home yet and I was getting help from the experts on the Camino forum to work out that crazy travel itinerary. Will I need more help, who knows, but at least I won't be afraid to ask if necessary.

I still had not worked out why I was doing this but something was calling me to get up of my fat ass and do something special. Hopefully over the next few weeks I would get my head around it and find a purpose for this mad, crazy adventure. In his Camino guide, John Brierley says we should have formulated our reasons before setting out but I am afraid that's just not me. If I were to sit around trying to work out 'why', I would never take that first step.

A year later as I write this, the reasons are still formulating in my mind. I am still finding reasons why and they mostly come back to a new relationship with Jesus, my family and my friends. Maybe when I have finished this journal I will have got my thoughts together well enough to add a chapter at the end or maybe not. Only time will tell.

But before I continue, what is this El Camino de Santiago?

El Camino de Santiago

The Camino de Santiago is an eight hundred kilometre trek or pilgrimage from the French foothills of the Pyrenees, across northern Spain to the resting place of the apostle, St James, and that was the sum total of my knowledge before undertaking my pilgrimage in 2013.

In Spanish he is Sant Iago or Sant Yago in the Galician tongue. Yago is closer to the other European translations of James as in Jacue or Jacob. It is thought that at some time in the distant past, the name of Santiago was split incorrectly as San Tiago giving rise to the Spanish name for James today, Diego.

There are many routes to Santiago but this one, the one I walked, known as the Camino Francés is the most popular. But how did it start, what are the origins? There are theories that there was a pre Christian Celtic route that went to Finisterre, long before the city of Santiago de Compostela was founded but the Christian pilgrimage is what I am concentrating on. Many authors will date it from the discovery of James' resting place but I prefer to think that it started with Jesus on the shores of the Sea of Galilee.

But first, why Spain? When we think of biblical times we tend to think only of Palestine, Greece and Rome, only the scholars think of the whole Mediterranean. It is as if nowhere else existed but by the time of Jesus' birth, the whole of the Mediterranean was part of what was called, the known world.

There is an old legend that the Iberian peninsula was once joined to Africa and became separated when the Phoenicians arrived and, having seen another great sea on the other side, decided to cut a canal allowing the Atlantic and Mediterranean to merge and change the sea levels thus leaving Egypt as dry land when it had been a shallow sea. Geologists tell us that yes, Egypt was under water, but the separation happened as the continents were being formed. I know the geologists are right but the old legend makes a better story.

The Phoenicians were a Semitic tribe and originated from northern Palestine or modern day Lebanon. They would also have been known as Canaanites and direct descendants of Noah. By 1100BC they had founded a city beyond the Pillars of Hercules (Gibraltar) called Gades, now Cadiz. The riches they discovered in the region attracted their rivals, namely Greeks, Babylonians, Assyrians and Persians. By 850BC the Phoenicians had founded another city this time on the North African coast, Carthage. About this time, the Assyrians were asserting their power in northern Palestine, striking at the Phoenician base and scattering the tribes of Israel who were under attack on two fronts, Assyrians in the north and the tribes of Judah in the south.

As the power of the Phoenicians declined at the hands of the Assyrians, the power of Carthage was on the rise but at the same time, to the north, a new power was growing, the Roman Republic. Inevitably these two great powers would clash and as the Iberian Peninsula was sandwiched between them, they clashed in Spain, the Punic wars between them being played out mostly on Spanish soil. By 45BC the world was on the brink of two momentous events. Julius Caesar had fought a civil war that gave birth to a new empire at the expense of the old republic. This empire would flourish and die in just a few centuries. The other event was the birth of Christianity.

Spain was therefore, by the time of Jesus, a well-known and thriving region of the Mediterranean world, inhabited by many peoples, both Semitic and gentile and of course that rare and unique people, the Basques who seem to have always been there.

The Tradition of Saint James

Against this background of power struggles in the Mediterranean was the simple and humble birth of Jesus, his ministry, death and resurrection.

Many millions of people in the 2000 years since Jesus walked this earth have chosen to hear his words and follow him but the first four, the eyewitnesses, the core group, were handpicked on the shore of the Sea of Galilee, Simon and his brother Andrew and James and his brother John. What made them so special that Jesus sought them out to be the first of millions? One reason may be that it has been said that James and John were first cousins of Jesus so maybe that is why they followed so readily. On the other hand these were men who were, more than likely, not just simple fishermen, but possibly, the small businessmen of the day. More can be read on this at *newadvent.org*. In January 1986, during a drought, the level of the Sea of Galilee dropped to reveal a fishing boat protruding from the mud. After excavation it was obvious from its size, 27ft(8.27m) long, 7.5ft(2.3m) wide and 4.4ft(1.3m) high that it would take more than one man to handle this vessel and its nets. It would have had four rowers and one helmsman and up to a possible 15 others so Simon must have been an employer as well. The Bible tells us that the first four apostles were partners so they may have had a lucrative business and been leaving behind a comparatively prosperous life but they were called and they followed.

During the short but eventful ministry of Jesus, these four were constantly at his side and apart from the crucifixion, were present at all the major events recorded in the Gospels. James and John were nicknamed by Jesus, Boanerges, the Sons of Thunder. When their mother, Salome, asked that her sons should sit at Jesus's left and right when he came into his kingdom, he said that that was not his gift to give but he warned that James would drink from the same cup, i.e. martyrdom. His death is the only one of the apostles recorded in the New Testament, however, the early church historian, Eusebius, has from his study of apocryphal writings told us that all but John suffered martyrdom for their belief in Jesus. John's calling was to care for the Virgin Mary until she died and then he lived to a very old age and wrote the book of *Revelations* or *the Apocalypse*. A 1st Century apocryphal gospel, *the Gospel of the 12 Apostles*, tells us that at Pentecost, each apostle received the language of the land in which they were to spread the good news. James got Latin which was the language of the western Mediterranean i.e. Spain. Around the 4th century a tradition had developed that believed that each apostle, on his death, was buried in the land wherein he had preached. Circa 600AD, 200 years before the discovery of his tomb, there was a document, The *Breviary of the Apostles* that tells us that James did indeed preach in Hispania and was buried in North West Spain close to the sea. Around 700AD, a poem, by the *Bishop of Sherborne* mentions James in Hispania. The *Commentary on the Apocalypse*, 785AD, lists the provinces of the world with its corresponding apostle and it lists James with Spain. In the same period a hymn, *O Dei Verbum Patris*, mentions the sons of thunder spanning the Mediterranean, John in Asia Minor and James in Spain. Could that be to the left and right where their mother Salome requested they should be? The hymn includes the lines

Oh most worthy and most holy apostle

Shining golden Chieftain of Spain

Be our protector and patron Saint on Earth

Warding off all ill

The above words are used to this day each time the Botafumeiro is swung. It is clear that there was a literary tradition in the early church that James preached in Spain and was buried there and this tradition predates the discovery of the tomb by 200 years. Another old tradition that developed after the discovery, tells us that while in Zaragoza, James had a vision from Mary calling him to return to Jerusalem to help stabilize the early church there. For his efforts he met his death by beheading at the hands of Herod Agrippa. As he went to his death, his executioner was so affected by James' courage in facing his fate that he declared he was a Christian and went to his death with James rather than executing him. Another account at *newadvent.org* says it was his accuser. Once again, James was called and once again he answered that call. By his death, he reiterated what he had seen during his life. He had seen and spoken to Jesus after his death on the cross. Would a man give his life for a lie he had been perpetrating? Doubtful. Would eleven men die horrible deaths rather than admit lying? Not a chance. Therefore, their deaths were tantamount to deathbed declarations that the resurrection was a very real event and Jesus was indeed the divine Son of God.

Herod would not allow James to have a Christian burial and had his body thrown into the street for the dogs, but his followers, Athanasius and Theodore, gathered up his body and decapitated head and took it to Jaffa on the coast where they set sail for Spain. Legend tells us it was in a stone boat carried on the wings of angels. It was more likely a stone sarcophagus to store the body during the long voyage to the North West coast of Spain. His body would have been transported by the descendants of the Phoenicians in one of their strong, cedar wood ships. These men would have been experienced at sailing into the Atlantic especially as, if legend is true, they did, in their day sail as far north as Cornwall and Ireland.

Athanasius and Theodore made land at Padrón near Finnisterre where the seven people James had converted were waiting and from there his body was borne by a team of oxen provided by a local queen, Lupa, to its final resting place in a marble tomb, also provided by the queen. Some legends say that Lupa was not very helpful and the burial took place despite her rather than because of her. This legend says she conspired with the Romans to destroy the body. However, the little band escaped with the body and after crossing a bridge over Rio Tambre, it collapsed thus preventing pursuit by their enemies. The body was laid to rest at Libredon, now Santiago. That Lupa converted to Christianity however does not seem to be in doubt. James' followers, Athanasius and Theodore would also be buried here eventually and then, the Son of Thunder and his final resting place would be forgotten for almost 800 years.

Before the Discovery of the Forgotten Tomb

Between the Apostle's burial and the discovery of the tomb, Spain witnessed the fall of the Roman Empire in the peninsula and the invasion of barbarian tribes over the Pyrenees; tribes like the Gauls and Visigoths. During their interminable squabbles, the Visigoths invited help from the Moors across the straits of Gibraltar in Morocco but this tactic, unfortunately for them and the Gauls, backfired and by 711AD, the Iberian Peninsula was dominated by Islam, just under 80 years after the death of Mohammed. Legend has it that the Moors carried a bone from his arm into battle thereby guaranteeing victory. In the north, the Muslim governor, Munuza demanded that the old Visigoth lords, who had been pushed back to the mountains where they were, for want of a better word, retired, pay him taxes. The lords of Asturias, led by Pelayo, rebelled, and defeated the moors at Covadonga. Although the moors would remain the major power in Spain for the next 500 years, this battle is considered the beginning of 'Reconquista'. This was also the beginning of the Kingdom of Asturias that would eventually be ruled by Alfonso II from 791 to 842 from his capitol at Oviedo.

The Moorish rule was not as one may think, a terrible time for those under their control. Unlike the Visigoths who tried to expel all Jews from the peninsula, the Moors were most benign and allowed complete freedom of religion. Science, art and architecture flourished under their rule and freely practising Christians built churches in the Moorish style. However, Christianity in Europe became very nervous when the Moorish rule eventually spread to the foothills of the Pyrenees. In 778AD Charlemagne, the Holy Roman Emperor, in an attempt to stop this advance, crossed the mountains from France, and laid siege to the city of Zaragoza, the same place James reputedly had his vision of the Blessed Virgin. After a month and with a ransom of gold he lifted the siege and started for home but, despite a promise to the Basques to the contrary, he attacked Pamplona on his return from the battle. This led in turn to the battle at Roncesvalles where his rear-guard, under the command of his nephew, Roland, was wiped out on the feast of the Assumption of the Blessed Virgin, Saturday August 15th. It is said that on a windy day, you can still hear the sound of Roland's horn, *Oliphant*, as he calls for help. Who was responsible though? Initially it was said the Basques ambushed them but later accounts say 400,000 Moors. This was possibly to glorify the defeat by claiming a superior force was responsible rather than admit the shame of an elite army being annihilated by a much inferior force of mountain tribesmen. It is more likely to have been the Basques because although fewer in numbers they would have had the advantage of fighting in a narrow mountain pass which suited them and not the heavily armoured knights. It is an argument that continues to modern times in that region of Navarre. The *Song of Roland or La Chanson de Roland* is one of the oldest surviving written documents in French literary history. It is tough going but worth it if you have the stamina to read it all.

By the year 800AD after Charlemagne's retreat, all of Spain was under Moorish rule with the exception of Asturias and Galicia, now under the rule of Alfonso II

The Discovery of the Tomb

According to legend, in the year 810 or 814 in some accounts, a Galician shepherd was led by a bright star to the burial site. The shepherd is known variously as Pelay, Paio or Pelayo. Is 'Pelayo' history confusing him with the hero of the same name who in 722 defeated the Moors? Regardless of his name, the discovery was confirmed as the grave of the apostle by the local Bishop of Iria Flavia, Theodomir. When the Bishop entered the tomb, he found, in a marble sarcophagus, a decapitated corpse with its head under its arm. Two other bodies were in the tomb and these were declared to be James' followers, Athanasius and Theodore. There was a stone with their names inscribed but not the name of James. I have read in another Camino book that there was a letter saying that it was the body of James but I can find no confirmation of this In any other writings. Alfonso II took up the cry and ordered the building of a Cathedral on the spot and declared Sant Iago, to be the patron saint of Spain. He then set of to visit the tomb along a Roman road known today as Camino Primitivo. News of the discovery soon made its way to France and to Louis the Pious at the Carolingian court at Aachen. This was possible as Asturias was not as one may think, cut off from the rest of Europe by the Moorish occupation. Communications by sea were possible and the old Roman road along the Cantabrian coast was still free to travel. Pilgrims from France were already using these routes to visit Oviedo to pray before the shrine of San Salvadore whose remains had been carried there by Visigoth churchmen fleeing the Moors. They also came to pray at the shrine of *Siete Varones Apostolicus*, seven youths who were said to have been followers of James.

The champion much needed by Christian Spain and bones to rival the bone of Mohammed had been found. The name given to the area was Campus for field and Stella for star or field of stars, Compostela.

In the year 844AD, James was said to have appeared on a white charger at the battle of Clavijo and slaughtered tens of thousands of Moors. He was also said to have made an appearance centuries later at a battle in South America between the natives and conquistadors. I find all this hard to believe from an apostle of Jesus who had heard Him in the Garden at Gethsemane denounce the use of the sword, but the legend grew, the legend of Santiago Matamoras, the Moor slayer, the legend that provided a battle cry for the Spanish forces. When many centuries later, Franco and his Moroccan (Moorish) army entered Santiago to dedicate themselves to Spain, all statues portraying the Moor Slayer had been discreetly covered up.

It did not however always go the way of the Spanish. In 997AD the Moors under the leadership of Al-Mansoor captured and sacked Santiago itself, but for some reason, he did not destroy or desecrate the grave of the apostle. The power of the Moors was not finally broken until 1212 at the battle of Las Navas de Tolosa. The Moors were finally defeated by Santiago and El Cid but El Cid is another story for another day. Once again James had been called to assist the church.

The Camino is Born

Against this back ground, the pilgrimage, the Camino, was born. News of the discovery was now spreading from Aachen to the rest of France and the first foreign pilgrim in 947 is said to have been the Bishop of Le Puy, Gotescalc. Although there is a route today from Le Puy to St Jean Pied de Port and thence on to the Camino Frances, the Bishop is unlikely to have used this way as the Meseta was still under the control of the Moors. He probably used the old Roman road along the coast following today's Camino del Norte. From the year 1000, the number of pilgrims started to increase, and in 1075 work started on the magnificent Romanesque cathedral which was consecrated in 1211. By the 11th Century Alfonso VI had added Galicia and Castile, and La Rioja and Navarre to his Leonese Kingdom thus creating a swath of land from the Pyrenees to the coast no longer in Moorish hands. He asked the Benedictine order to set up a chain of houses along the Roman roads in places like Irache, Nájera, Sahagún, Astorga and O'Cebreiro. Roads and bridges were built by Santo Domingo De La Calzada, St Dominic in English. The Camino Frances was born. (*Much of the above information was made available by the British confraternity at 'csj.org.uk'*) The Christian world now had three great pilgrimage routes, Rome, Jerusalem and Santiago. As Jerusalem faded in popularity due to the dangers of travel during and after the crusades, Santiago became more and more popular. The Knights Templar, who traditionally protected the pilgrim on his way to Jerusalem, turned their attention to Spain and their influence can still be seen along the modern Camino, especially in Ponferrada where there is a perfectly preserved Templar Castle. Hospitaller knights started setting up hospitals or refugios to care for the medieval peregrino and their influence can be seen in the towns called Hospital. By the end of the 13th century, Santiago had grown six fold in size and the number of pilgrims was in the many tens of thousands. They came in their long brown robes, a broad brimmed hat pinned back at the front and their bordons (wooden staffs) with a little bag with all their worldly possessions attached. With them they carried the scallop shell. This shell or '*coquille de Saint Jacques*' became the symbol of the Saint and the pilgrimage. There are as many legends about the shell as there are about the pilgrimage itself. The shells are plentiful along the coast and some say the pilgrims picked them up as souvenirs to prove they had walked the extra miles to Finnisterre. Another tale tells of how, a young noble man, having fallen into the sea, prayed to Saint James to save him and on emerging safely from the water, he was covered in shells. Another and more probable reason is the fact that the shell could be used to scoop up water and its rough edge could be used to cut food. Whatever the tale, to this day, many Spaniards do not carry the shell to Santiago, they only carry them away at the end of the journey.

The ideal date to arrive in Santiago is the Saints feast day, July 25th. If it falls on a Sunday it is declared a Holy Year and during that year only, the Puerta Santa or Holy Door is open for pilgrims to enter the Cathedral. For the Holy year of 2004, almost 180,000 pilgrims collected their compostelas. The next Holy year will be 2021 and I will be 72 and if God spares me I might give it a go.

Each day, as the pilgrims arrive, there is a pilgrim mass at noon. It has become something of a tourist attraction now and more often than not the pilgrim has to stand while the tourists sit. In the past, the giant botafumeiro was swung on special days but nowadays it can be any day if there is a group prepared to pay the Cathedral authorities for the privilege. Traditionally, the purpose of the incense was to cover the smell of thousands of unwashed medieval pilgrims who did not have the privilege of showers like the modern day peregrino.

The next part of the pilgrimage for the medieval pilgrim must have been a real downer. Unlike the modern day pilgrim, he now had to turn and walk all the way back home. No trains or boats or planes for him.

[15]

The Peregrinos

But what about the pilgrims? Who were they, who are they and why do they keep coming in their tens of thousands? All kinds made the journey, the rich, the poor, the criminal and the clergy, even Saint Francis, but mostly, the poor, the peasants, the serfs. Often, the serf would be the proxy walker for the nobility, sometimes even the proxy for the criminal. During the Holy Year the pilgrim would receive a plenary indulgence that would excuse them from doing any time in purgatory. In other years they would only get half their time off. In some countries, particularly the Netherlands, convicted criminals could have their sentence commuted by walking the Camino. I don't know when this practice died out but I did read somewhere that it was still on the statute books. Today's pilgrim comes for many reasons; 'retreat', a way to get closer to God, a way to 'sort out their heads', a way to find themselves or just the plain old adventure of the long distance hike. There may be those seeking a cure but personally, I have not heard any tales of curative powers associated with the Camino. There may be, I just have not come across any. Some Spanish do it, as it is good to have on a CV when looking for a job. The one thing they all have in common is that they are much better equipped for the journey than the pilgrim of old and the accommodation is much more available as is the food, by way of the tasty and cheap '*menu de peregrino*' offered by almost every small bar and restaurant along the way. It is a tough trek but compared to yesteryear, it's a walk in the park. They came and continue to come from every country in the world and from every faith and no faith and they are all joined by a common phrase, '*Buen Camino*'.

The Death of the Camino

But nothing lasts forever. In the 16th century, the Camino began to die. The Black Plague was ravaging the continent, the rise of Protestantism and European wars took a great toll on the numbers walking. Luther openly preached against Santiago.

> 'We do not know if James is buried there,
>
> A dog or a dead horse? Then do not go.'

A little known event dealt it a hammer blow. The pirate, Francis Drake had announced that he would sack the city of Santiago and remove the body. When he raided La Coruña, the Archbishop, Don Juan de San Clemente, fearing the relics would fall into the hands of Protestant England, opened the tomb and removed the bones to a safe hiding place. Unfortunately, he hid them so well that when he died before revealing the hiding place the Saints body once again was 'lost', this time for 300 years. Once it became known that the shrine was empty, the number of pilgrims decreased to just a trickle. On the feast of St James in 1867 only a few dozen pilgrims turned up.

The Rebirth

On January 28th, 1879 during redecoration work in the Cathedral, workers pierced a vault hidden in the wall behind the main altar and there, in a container, they found the missing relics. The bones were confirmed as those of James when a jawbone that had been donated to a cathedral, Pistoia in Italy, centuries before, was compared to the skull they had found and they matched. In a letter, 'Deus Omnipotens' Pope Leo XIII announced the discovery and declared the remains to be St James. From that time on, the pilgrimage started to revive but very slowly. During the Napoleonic times soldiers tramped across the fields to do battle rather than the gentle pilgrim. As Europe continued to suffer political unrest, it was impossible to walk across the continent safely. The 20th Century brought the First World War followed by Spanish flu and then the rise of fascism. Spain was rent in two by the fascist forces of Franco and armoured vehicles were on the Meseta, not peregrinos. During the reign of Franco tens of thousands disappeared at the hands of his secret police to be tortured and buried in mass graves, especially in the region of Valencia. Spain was not a very welcoming destination. Even when in November 1975, Franco died and Spain was opening up more and more to the tourist, the Camino was still in hibernation. After the Falangist rebellion in Spain the world was ravaged by the Second World War and the greatest evil thrown up by fascism, the Nazis. It was hard enough to be able to survive in your own home without facing the dangers of evil dictators in Germany, Italy and Spain.

On 14th May 2005, in Toronto, an address was given to a gathering of Pilgrims by *Laurie Dennett,* former chairman of *the British Confraternity,* and it is published in full on their web site *www.csj.org.uk*. They give permission for the reproduction of material so a lot of what follows is thanks to them and *Laurie Dennett*.

As mentioned earlier, the result of wars ravaging Europe detracted from the numbers on Camino but coincidently, those wars coincided with Holy Years. It was not until 1948 that a Holy Year was widely publicised outside Spain.

The first response was in France where a group of historians set up '*Societe des Amis du Chemin de Saint Jacques*', society of the friends of the way of St James. To this day many confraternities use this formula of 'the friends of St James'.

[18]

The French 'Amis' filmed their journey to Santiago in 1949 and when it went on French TV in 1950 it resulted in many French pulling on their boots and heading out on the Camino.

In the Holy Year of 1965 a Spanish version of 'Amis' was formed in Estella and in 1969 they published maps and a guidebook, although the book was a bit large and heavy to carry with you. The maps were not of the route the French took however; they had followed mainly Franco's roads. The scholars in Estella had actually delved into the archives and found the old trails that were at that time just farmland tracks used only by the farmers.

In the Holy Year 1971, a Galician priest, Don Elias Valiña Sampredo, having restored the church and village of O' Cebreiro, produced a smaller guide book that could fit easily in the pocket. Having built up a network of people along the Way, he gave the Camino something that would ensure it never died out again. He way marked the entire route with the much loved yellow arrows or 'flechas amarilla'. Those reassuring little arrows that say 'Don't worry peregrino, you are not lost'. To this day along the Camino, the local people continue to keep those arrows well painted.

By 1987, there were confraternities in Italy, Germany, Belgium, the Netherlands and Britain. Once again James had been called upon to revive the Camino and through these confraternities set up in his name in many lands, the numbers began to grow again, slowly but surely. Also in 1987, just after Spain had joined the EEC, the route was designated as the first European Cultural Route and new bright blue and yellow waymarks started to appear alongside the arrow and the Camino began to see the coach tours and guided walking holidays for what we laughingly called, the 'touregrinos'.

In 1991 the 10,000 pilgrims' barrier was broken.

Holy Year 1993 almost 100,000

1999   153,000

2004   180,000

Holy Year 2010   272,000

2012   198,000

[19]

Other factors like the accessibility of air travel to the ordinary man and the excellent train and bus services within Europe have helped greatly. The author, *John Brierley*, through his definitive *'Pilgrims Guide to the Camino de Santiago'* has in his own way helped many to pull on their boots and just walk. As he says, '*don't forget to start*'. Another author, *Hape Kerkeling* in his book, *'I'm Off Then'* inspired many German speakers, and when it was translated into English it helped inspire me. For a time after the publication of this book, Germans were the predominant nationality on the Camino. The final spur to restore the Camino to its former glory was delivered by Hollywood. Emilio Estevez and his father Martin Sheen made the movie *'The Way'* and today, many pilgrims are inspired by it to travel to Spain and complete their own 'Way'. Estevez was inspired by his father who had completed a part of the Camino in 2003 and suggested his son should make a movie about it. It took five years to find a script they both liked but at last they were happy with what they had and the movie was made. To the best of my knowledge however, Martin Sheen, has not done it in its entirety.

Some interesting facts

The botafumeiro first appeared in the 13ᵗʰ century. It was replaced by one made of silver presented by Louis XI. This was stolen by Napoleon's army during the Peninsular war and never seen again. The next one was an iron copy. The present one, installed in 1851 is of silvered brass. Some say it is the biggest in the world and some say it is second to one in Oldenburg, Germany.

The Holy Doors, sometimes known as Puerta Del Perdón in the Praza de la Quintana are only open in Holy Years. Puerta del Perdón or door of pardon is called this as pilgrims passing through it get full remission for their sins.

In Nordic sagas, Galicia is known as 'Jackobsland'.

But now, back to my story

My Pilgrimage

Belfast to Pamplona

Well it's now the Friday night before we go, 15th March. I just need to decant my tablets for my diabetes and arrange a taxi to get us to Belfast International for 4:30am to check in for the first leg of our journey to Biarritz via London Stansted. Will the gods throw anything else at us between now and our arrival in Pamplona? I hope not. All I know for sure is that we will be in Iruña, the Basque name for Pamplona in time for St Patrick's Day.

It's the 16th and time to go. My daughter Sarah, God love her, has volunteered to drive us to the airport and has got up at 3:30am on a cold icy morning, a sign of things to come, if only we had known. I am about to head off into the unknown. Every journey I have ever made in my life has had one thing in common. I have always known where I would be laying down my head for the night. I don't know for sure where the hostel is or if there will even be any beds. I have no comfort blanket on this journey and I head into it with some trepidation. But for now, the flights are all good. EasyJet asked us to sit in the extra legroom seats as they can't take off if there is no-one by the emergency exit to open it if need be so we were able to really stretch out. After a long boring layover in Stansted it was finally time for our Ryanair flight to Biarritz. We took the first seats we came to after boarding the jet at the rear but others who rejected those seats in favour of finding better ones further forward ended off being split up, so once again a bit of comfort and a window seat again. We arrived in Biarritz on schedule at 4pm local time after a comfortable flight. The trains to Hendaye and on to San Sebastian were, with continental efficiency, on time. We met an English girl whose name I forget who was planning to stay in Donostia/San Sebastian in some language school scheme to learn some Spanish before heading out on the Camino. At the station, we had to say goodbye to her as time was shorter than we had planned, so we must run to try to get to the station for the early bus but, unfortunately, we did not make it so it had to be the late bus to Pamplona at 20:30. If we had made it that's the time we would have been arriving rather than setting out. It was a pleasant evening until the sun went down but it got quite cold by the time the bus arrived. While we were waiting, I got my first taste of churros, very sweet so probably not good for a diabetic so I never tried them again. At last, we were on the bus for Pamplona. It's dark but we could

[22]

see enough through the window to realise just how much snow there was at these fairly low levels. I was so glad we didn't try to negotiate the Pyrenees.

We arrived in Pamplona at about 22:00. The plan to get something to eat in the bus station did not happen as everywhere was closed so we headed directly for Hostel Hemingway. Following my own written instructions, I got confused on a very large roundabout and missed my turning as I was counting the exits re our clockwise roundabouts at home forgetting that continental ones go anti-clockwise. There was an old man standing in a shop doorway so, much as I feared trying to converse in a foreign language, I approached him and with some broken Spanish, asked the way to Calle Amaya. I must have been able to communicate my problem OK as he understood and pointed us in the right direction. Finally we arrived in the Hostel about 22:30, got two beds in a shared dorm and settled down for a well-earned sleep. It had been a long day that had taken me out of my comfort zone as far as travelling is concerned, but we got here in the end. It's a good Hostel by the way, I would certainly recommend it.

Buenos Noches y Buen Camino

St Patrick's Day in Pamplona

Day One, Sunday 17th March,

At last, the day we were to start walking has arrived, St Patrick's Day, but we have decided to wait until the 18th and just have a good rest in Pamplona. After breakfast, supplied by the Hostel, we found the church of St Anthony just around the corner and Mass is just about to begin. We were lost last night and I can't help thinking he found us and guided us here via the Hostel.

After Mass we walked through the town and found the statue dedicated to the *Running of the Bulls*. Something is wrong with my camera as the automatic lens cover will only open halfway. Am I going to have to rely on my phone camera? After a few sharp taps, it opens and seems to be OK. We took a few photos then made our way to the Jesus y Maria Albergue, signed in and got our first Sello or pilgrim stamp. By the way, regarding cameras, Chris forgot to bring his but remembered his tripod, so he will have to depend on his phone. We are still dreaming about the KFC we didn't get last night so we make our way round to the bus station. On the way we spot what looks like a political party meeting in a conference hall so for a laugh I go and mingle in among the crowd. Chris is not best pleased about it, I think I embarrassed him. After a good lunch, where I discovered that the Spanish do not understand 'Diet' Coke, (its Coke light), we made our way back to an Irish bar we had found earlier. Now, I am not a great one for looking for Irish bars while away, but it is St Patrick's Day so in we go and get a couple of Guinness. Is it just that I am thirsty or is it about the

[24]

best Guinness I have ever tasted? What a laugh. The only Irishmen, in an Irish pub, on St Paddy's Day in Pamplona, but the Spanish are all wearing some sort of Irish regalia. Fortunately I have brought my 'Wolfe Tones' scarf so I can wear our colours.

The day is drawing to an end so we must get dinner before it gets too late so we head for a restaurant that does 'menu de peregrino'. Just our luck, it's closed, so we end up in the famous Café Iruña, a favourite of Ernest Hemingway when he lived here. Good food, good service and good wine, if not a little strong and all for €13 each. One of the other customers is Saint Patrick. Even the Spanish have a parade with someone dressed as our patron Saint. Back in the albergue its 21:15 and I am in bed. Haven't been to bed this early since I was a child but all in all it's been a great St Patrick's Day and there is hard walking waiting for us in the morning.

Buenos Noches y Buen Camino

Pamplona to Puente la Reina

Or how I only made it to Uterga

Day Two, Monday, March 18th

Today is a 24Km hike as long as we don't take any detours. This will be my first test of walking with a back pack and I have never walked this far before. In fact I have never walked half that far but it is too late to worry about it now. The walk from Pamplona to Cizur Menor in the early morning gloom is not too bad although I developed a pain in my right thigh that only seems to bother me going downhill. After we had passed the university district, Chris told me that he had heard that if you get a sello from every university along the way, you are entitled to an honorary degree from Santiago University. If he had mentioned it earlier we could have found out but I am not turning back on an off chance that it may be true. At Cizur Menor we stopped at a little pub Christopher had found the previous year and I get to taste my first café con leche grande. I am amazed to find it is served in a glass tumbler but it tastes like no coffee I have ever tasted in my life and it helps to warm my hands as I cup them round the glass, it's still early enough in the year for chilly mornings, even in Spain.

The hill up to the first town, Zariquiegui, is not too steep but I am finding it difficult. Along the way we are overtaken by 'Girls on the Way', a mother and two daughters, the eldest just 12, who have walked from St Jean through many feet of snow. I had read about them on the Camino forum and as we chat for a couple of minutes the eldest girl, when she realises we are Irish, wishes us a happy St Patrick's Day even though it was yesterday. Two lovely, well-mannered kids, who will walk a heck of a lot more kilometres than I will. We will not meet them again but I will follow the mother's blog on their progress all the way to Finisterre. An elderly Japanese man and a young man called Jan from Slovenia catch up on us and after a short stop for a chat, move on. Jan is carrying far too much in his back pack but who am I to talk, mine is also too heavy but nothing like his. Mine is also for some reason hanging to the left and causing me some pain in my left shoulder. I never solved this problem and it was still hurting when I reached Santiago. The ruck sack was the only thing I scrimped on and bought cheap. A big mistake. Anyway, we stop in a little garden in the town for something to eat and I feel refreshed with some food in me and a compliment from two young men who say I am doing well for

[26]

my age, so off we go again to make the ascent to the summit. The scenery is great, the walk is tough but it looks like we will make it without too much difficulty. Looks can be deceiving and in this case that's exactly what they are. As we reach the top of a little crest we find an almost sheer drop of about 2 meters in deep slippery mud. The wooden steps that used to be here are lying in a heap at the bottom of the slope. Can we make it down with our walking poles dug in deep? I can't see any other way but just then, another peregrino, coming up behind us says he has spotted another path that will take us around it so we back track and it brings us out at the bottom of the slope where we want to be. But now we are very tired and walking almost constantly in deep mud that drags at our feet and legs and makes each step an agony and then we reach another obstacle, even deeper mud. To the left we can go up through a field in deep snow but is there a way back to the trail? We can't see for sure. We could go down to the right but the path there is blocked by a briar patch. Much as I dislike the idea, the briar patch is the best bet for getting through. At this point two Australian girls, Robin and Amanda catch up on us and I help them through the briars by holding bushes back with my walking poles. We will meet both of them again. I have really suffered on this ascent but at last we make the top, bitterly cold, boots and trousers covered in mud, a severe pain in my right thigh but at least it's all downhill from here. A child's broken toboggan provides a few shards of plastic that we can use to scrape clean the soles of our boots so that the grips are visible again ready for the descent. I check my blood sugar levels before starting and everything is ok.

The descent is short, but steep and treacherous over loose scree and by the time we reach the bottom I am completely exhausted. There is nothing left in my tank, but there is no choice, I must keep putting one foot in front of the other. I start to use a technique that will help me on many hills yet to come. I pick a spot ahead and focus on that spot, and that spot only, as my goal and then rest when I reach it. It could be a rock or a bush or just simply a tuft of grass. There is no way I will make it to Puente la Reina today. Just outside Uterga there is a small grotto to the Blessed Virgin and I stop and sit down for a chat with her. Get me to that white wall about 50 meters away and then I will ask for the next 50 is what I say to her. Well she got me to that wall and beyond down into the green at the top of the town. Chris knows that I have reached my limit so he leaves me sitting on a raised concrete manhole cover while he goes on into town to check if the albergue is open. I ask Mary and her Son to please let it be open. Am I getting religious? My phone rings, its Chris with the news it is open and he is coming back to carry my back pack the rest of the way into town. As I stagger into the bar, Robin and Amanda are waiting to greet me and offer me a drink to revive me. They will never know how much that meant to me.

It's a bit more expensive than other albergues but it includes dinner and breakfast. After a slightly embarrassing shower (I was in the ladies without realising it but fortunately no one came in) I feel a little better but a bit light headed. I check my blood sugar and it's the lowest I have seen it, 4.8. A bit of chocolate will sort that and outside sitting in the sun will make me feel better. At this point two Americans arrive. Gerry, from Jacksonville, Florida, and his good friend, Mike from Virginia. They both served together in the US Navy as young men and are still good friends in later life. I would guess they are both in their mid to late fifties. Two lovely guys that we will meet again. After a marvellous three course dinner I feel so much better, the company is great and we chat and get to know a little about each other over a glass or two of vino.

Tomorrow will be a short day as we will walk the last 7km to Puente la Reina, book into the Hotel Jakue albergue, get our washing done and recuperate. I really need to get my backpack sorted. It's too heavy and lop sided. It is 21:15 and I am going to bed but at least there will be no early morning start as breakfast is served at 8:30 in this marvellous albergue.

This day over Mont Perdón, or mud-slide Mountain as we will hear it described later, has been physically, the toughest day of my life and I hope I never have to face an ordeal like that again. Unfortunately, there will be another day just as bad, but for now, I can't conceive of there ever being another. However it is behind me and I do feel a little bit of pride that I actually had the strength and will power to force myself to take each step when my whole being was screaming, enough is enough. I am discovering an inner strength that I didn't know I had. A couple of years ago, if I had known about it, I would have considered the Camino to be a fool's quest. Walking to the top of the street to catch a bus once or twice a year was about as much as I would have considered doing and here I am with 17.5Km, about 10 miles, behind me which included walking to the top of a small mountain. Didn't quite make the 24km I started out to do though but maybe that was a little ambitious given my lack of fitness.

Well tomorrow is another day and another challenge

Buenos Noches y Buen Camino

Uterga to Puente La Reina

Or how we pushed on to Mañeru

Day Three, Tuesday, 19th March

Today we start out for Puente La Reina after a good breakfast in the Albergue Perdón. Everyone is up and ready to go except Gerry who eventually arrives downstairs, still in his night attire with no intentions of hurrying himself to go anywhere. I christen him '*last man lying*' and he earns that reputation on other days yet to come. After saying our goodbyes, we set off at a brisk pace that lasts all of five minutes with me then it is back to my normal snail pace. It's an easy trek and had I been able to carry on last night we could have made Puente La Reina easily. Before we know what is happening we are standing in front of the Hotel Jakue that has an albergue at the back. We had planned on staying here but it's far too early to stop and I still feel quite good so we decide to have a mid-morning snack and some more of that wonderful coffee. As we sit enjoying our second breakfast, along come Mike and Gerry but they don't stop for long and off they go. Our boots are laced up again and off we go through the old town and there, sitting under the town gate enjoying a snack and a beer, are our two American friends. We bid them Buen Camino and press on. Outside of town, it really is a must to stop and admire the old bridge, Puente La Reina, from which the town takes its name, and take some photos.

At this point there is a wide road to cross but it is not busy so over we go and set off down a lane following the ever present yellow arrows. We will grow to love those yellow arrows as they say, '*don't worry pilgrim; someone else has done this before you*'. Ahead we see another peregrino in a green jacket. He holds back till we catch up and as we chat I realise he is the '*big green egg*' whom I chatted with on the forum before we left. He has like me, a bit of a belly making him egg shaped, his jacket is green hence the handle. It's real muddy along this stretch, not from rain but from some industrial work going on. I realise I am walking faster than I can handle to keep up with the '*egg*' so I tell him to go on as I am only slowing him down. We bid him farewell, we never met him again.

The path now winds through some open countryside and in the distance we can see a couple of storks standing motionless in a field. Chris wonders what they must be thinking so I offer a suggestion, '*would you look at those two daft Irishmen staring at us wondering what we are thinking*'. The trail now runs parallel with the N-111 for a short while and starts to rise quite steeply to meet the road and I am afraid, I do not do hills well. There is a slight burning sensation in my left foot, so fearing the start of a blister; the boots come off for an inspection. Nothing seems wrong but I change my socks for my Marino wool ones I bought just before leaving and while I sit there tending to my feet and Chris is off playing around at a stream like a big kid, along come Mike and Gerry again. It's not the first time they have overtaken us and it won't be the last. At the crest of the hill we are at a roundabout looking down at the village of Mañeru. I am feeling tired and the Brierley guide says there is an albergue here, Albergue Lurgorri, so we decide to stop here for the night. Unfortunately, it's locked and looks like it will stay that way. Oh well, looks like it will have to be a plod on to Cirauqui but it's on top of a pretty steep hill. My left foot is hurting again so we walk a few metres back to the town fountain and rest up on a park bench to get some Vaseline on my foot. I didn't believe this would be any good but it really works. As I work it into my foot, some guy comes riding by on a bike, circles around a bit and then takes down a patio chair from a stack outside the albergue, lights a cigarette and sits back and watches us. '*Are you opening the albergue*' I ask and to our delight he nods in the affirmative. In we go to find a long dining room, office and a computer with free Wi-Fi. Our host offers us dinner and breakfast for a small charge and we gratefully accept. He shows us to the sleeping quarters and they look clean and cosy. We have struck lucky again. There is a washing area out the back with a clothes line to hang our washing on. Bad idea. The little courtyard is so sheltered it gets no sun so there is little drying as my Mum used to say. To make matters worse, there is something wrong with the heating so the radiators never come on to dry our clothes on. Well, so much for expensive fast drying trousers. My Expedition shirt dried out overnight but the trousers did not.

I now become the keeper of the Albergue Lurgorri. Our host Koldo, his Basque name, or Luis, his Spanish name must go out and as the doors lock automatically, he chooses me as the key holder for the night as he does not sleep on the premises. It has been a fairly good day, big improvement on yesterday and I don't feel like my tank is completely empty. Unfortunately our American and Australian friends have pushed on past this town so I doubt I will see them again. I feel a little sad about that but the Camino comes up with some strange things and we do indeed meet all four again.

At dinner we met a Swiss lady called Cecilia. She spoke many languages but unfortunately very little English. She has walked all the way from her home in Switzerland and proudly shows us her credentials. She is amazed to learn that we do not teach our children another language in primary school, but, I point out that we don't even teach them our own language, Irish, so technically our kids are taught a foreign language. With a smattering of school French, a few Spanish words, some English and a lot of signs we managed to communicate and enjoyed a marvellous dinner with some very nice vino tinto. We had boiled asparagus laid out in the shape of the Camino shell with cream and tuna as the base of the shell. It doesn't sound very good but it was delicious. This was followed by a large serving of Spanish meatballs with wine. Hard to finish but I insisted on everyone having a second helping rather than leave so much in case our host would feel offended. He was a really nice guy and I would not have wanted to hurt his feelings. Tomorrow our goal is Estella. I think we can make that OK but for now sleep is what we need so bed by 9:30 again

Buenos Noches y Buen Camino

Mañeru to Estella

Day Four, Wednesday, 20th March

After a good breakfast supplied by Koldo we set off at about 9am, just in time to see Cecilia disappear into the distance. The next town, Cirauqui, is just a short distance ahead, 3Km, but it sits on top of a hill. We stopped at a little shop to buy some yoghurt which tasted like the best yoghurt in the world at the time. Although the ascent through the town is not much more than 50m, some of the streets are almost straight up and an old woman, clearly many years older than me, passed us by, quite funny that, but it helped to keep me going. At the top of the town there is a desk with another Sello to collect so we stopped to stamp our pilgrim passports before moving on. As we come out the other side of the town and start descending across an old ruined Roman bridge, Chris spots a strange sight. Across the valley, someone has laid out a massive map of the world using old tyres. Some farmer has too much time on his hands but we stop to take photos of it.

The day is turning into a nice one. The sun has come out but not too warm, just nice for hiking. There are still some very wet and muddy patches as we descend into the valley of the Rio Salado. In places there is just enough dry ground for walking in single file. Of course, that just would have to be where other walkers are catching up with me and want past. Most wait their turn but one guy is so impatient he charges through the deep mud and water. Oh well, that's his problem. At this point a number of Asians who turn out to be Korean start to pass us, when one girl stops dead in her tracks and asks if we are Irish. She has been living and studying in Dublin for the last year. We exchange a few words then off she goes. As we reach the river

[33]

valley bottom I just have to stop for a rest and some water and as the ground is dry, I drop my rucksack and sit down on the path between an underpass and a road crossing. Two elderly ladies and an old man come around the bend from under the underpass and the old man is hobbling along using a large pole for support and smoking. This guy is not only old but he smokes too and he looks fitter than me. 'Poco Poco' he says with a smile as he passes, along with the customary 'Buen Camino'. Seems this means to take it easy, a little bit at a time. I pull myself up, shoulder my back pack and move on. Round the bend is an old bridge and the old man has stopped here for a rest and as I go past he repeats his earlier phrase. The Rio Salada is a raging torrent. The melting snows have all the rivers the same and we will see quite a few more in full flow that were just streams when Chris was here last year. Every valley unfortunately has two sides so now we must ascend the other side up to the town of Lorca. Along the way we are overtaken by Maurice from Malta. This is his second time on the Camino. Seems his family came originally from the north of Ireland but his accent sounds as if we are speaking with Sean Connery. Off he goes and I struggle on. I really am having difficulty with inclines.

We are becoming conscious of the fact that my pace is leaving us with a race against siesta every day. If we don't make it to Lorca soon, the shops will be closed and we have no food with us for lunch and breakfast seems like it is light years behind us.

I am starting to take notice of the dogs along the way. They are most definitely not pets and in many cases not very well looked after, they are guard dogs and look so emaciated that if set free might mistake me for a nice plump dinner. At this point I must say that when Chris was on the Camino last year I read a couple of books that warned the reader about rough terrain, thieves and wild dogs roaming the Camino. The only truth in that is the rough terrain. I never saw a wild dog anywhere. In fact the only wildlife I seen was a few storks and a dead owl. And there are no bands of marauding thieves, a few con men, but no thieves. In the cities there will be pickpockets but they seem to be in every city the world over. However I digress, as we enter the town, we pass a house with a well-kept garden and behind the hedge and railings is an Alsatian dog. It comes over to the hedge and pushes its face through a hole and makes a little whining noise that says, 'I am a good friendly dog.' I know it's a risk, but very gingerly, I reach out my hand and stroke his head. No risk, this really is a friendly dog. As we move on he runs to the bottom of the garden and is waiting at another hole for some more affection. I hated leaving him but we must make it to the local shop for food before siesta. We pass by a couple of albergues but they are not open for business until Easter which is next week but the owner who is working at cleaning the place up points us to the local shop. We find a patio table to sit at and Chris goes for food and drink. I notice Maurice sitting at another table at the far side of the yard with two young fellas and one calls out, 'Hi Irish'. Turns out he is from Kilkenny. He is called Tom and we will meet him a few more times. Two more pilgrims arrive and ask if they can share our table. One is Fernandez from Brazil but I have forgotten the name of his companion. Fernandez has very good English so he translates everything for his friend. As we start our meal we hear the click as the owner turns the lock and closes up for siesta, we just made it. About ten minutes later a car pulls up and a guy gets out and tries the door. I reckon it's fair enough if I don't know about siesta but you would think the locals would be well used to it. Eventually everyone starts moving on so we find ourselves sitting on our own and boy, did I want to sit there all day, but, there is nothing else for it because there is nowhere to stay in Lorca so like it or not we must push on to Estella. The sun has come out now so it is getting quite hot making the walk more difficult.

We, or should I say, I, struggle into Villatuerta. There are a lot of signs of the worldwide recession here. House after house is empty and up for sale and they are not old houses, some are very nice detached villas with large gardens.

Pavement walking is no fun at all but at least we can walk on the shady sides of the streets as we make our way through town. One shop is open even though it is still siesta and I make a big mistake. I am sick of drinking water so I buy a Coke light. The fizzy drink bubbles around my stomach and makes me feel unwell and uncomfortable. I won't make that mistake again. Hiking and fizzy drink do not go together.

At last Estella pops up from behind a hill and we descend into the town, Poco Poco, ha ha. Into the albergue, Hospital de Peregrinos, but if I want a bottom bunk I will have to go up stairs to the second floor. It may as well have been Everest for I had to use my walking poles to make it to the top. Once that back pack was off and I had a nice shower everything seemed a lot better. But now for dinner. A Portuguese guy in the foyer pointed us to a restaurant that had menu de peregrino. Seems he used to live on the Lisburn Rd in Belfast so we stop for a chat and he tells us that he was amazed at how tourists were allowed to scramble over the Giants Causeway and that he thought it should be protected more. I wonder did he come back to Ireland and tell them to charge exorbitant rates for the car park to keep people out. Nothing to do with my Camino, but must say that the Giants Causeway is the biggest rip off anywhere on the island of Ireland, but that's another story for another day.

The restaurant is just a handful of metres up the street and I get to try trout a la Navarre. They cut the tail off but leave the head on, strange. Never have I tasted fish quite as good though. Fernandez arrives and joins us for dinner. Back to the albergue and we run into Tom having dinner with the Korean girl from Dublin. We are developing a nice little group of friends now. Well fed, rested and cleaned up, it's time for bed. A bit late tonight, 9:30 instead of 9:15, such devils we are

5 days In Spain and counting

Buenos Noches y Buen Camino

Estella to Los Arcos

Day Five, Thursday, 21st March

It's an early start today but even though we started before 8am there are pilgrims already on the road. The first stop today is Irache with its famous wine fountain.

At last, a reason to use the tin cups I had such difficulty sourcing in Belfast, except Chris decides to use his scallop shell instead. As we sit enjoying a very early morning wine who comes up the hill but our two American compadres Mike and Gerry. How did we get in front of them again? They were ahead of us when we stopped in Mañeru. Turns out they stopped just ahead of us at Ciraqui and as Gerry tends to be in no hurry to get up in the morning, we probably passed them there and were on a different floor to them in the albergue in Estella. True to form we would have left before Gerry was up and now they are catching up on us again. As we enjoy a little more wine and take some photos a guy in a Stetson style hat comes up the hill and Gerry jokes that he is probably from Texas. Well he is, and we have now met Jim Cashion, henceforth to be known as Big Jim. He is walking with his daughter Caitlin and her friend Katie. He was supposed to be doing this with his wife who studied in Santiago in her student days but something had come up to prevent her coming with him. He plans to meet her in Sarria and they will finish the Camino together. To our surprise, Jim pours the water from his bottle and fills it with the wine. It's nice wine but water is better for you while hiking. At last all the socialising is over and everyone resumes the business of the day, walking to Los Arcos. We keep pace with Jim and his girls, who he refers to as K1 and K2, but as usual the first little hill we come to, I fall behind and Jim et al head of into the distance. The Way now winds through some pleasant rolling hills with great landscapes on the horizon so we stop for some photos before hiking on to the next town, Azqueta. A quiet, sleepy little town, where nothing is stirring except two crazy Irish peregrinos. It must be siesta. In that case we may as well join them and it seems like as good a place as any to stop for a rest and fill our bottles from the local fountain. Ahead is a very prominent looking hill with a building on top, a castle as far as I know. Do we have to climb that I wonder? Fortunately the answer is no, not to the top anyway, just a little way up, before dropping down into Villamayor de Monjardín.

Sitting comfortably in the square, drinking the last of his Irache wine is Big Jim and the girls. It's time to eat and even though it's still siesta the local bar is open so its café con leche time. We are joined shortly by Rick, another American, and two Canadian girls, Sarah and Kathleen. This is our first experience of tapas. As everyone has purchased something, the barman supplies free snacks including a bowl of black olives. May as well try them and I am pleasantly surprised at how good they are. Only problem is they are not pitted and I nearly break a tooth to everyone's amusement. It's a lovely afternoon but as the sun moves and leaves us in the shade we realise it is still early in the year and there is still a bit of a nip in the air. Simple solution, lift the whole table and move it back into the sun. I wondered if the bar owner was getting worried as he watched his table move further and further away from his bar. Just after 2pm a man approaches to tell us that the albergue is now open and ready for business. Jim, his family and Rick have been waiting for this as they had already decided to stay here. I considered it but, as the weather was good for walking, it was early in the day and I had had a good rest with excellent company and, feeling on top of the world, I decide to push on to Los Arcos. Won't be feeling on top of the world when I get there but I will get there. The Canadian girls say they are in no hurry so will be taking it easy as they are just oot and aboot (sorry Canada). A mile or two along the way they go shooting past us. Is that taking it easy Canadian style?

What a boring walk, flat with no landmarks of any kind. Mile after mile, walking between fields and vineyards not yet in bloom. Vineyards this early in the year look like dead stumps, not pleasant to look at. The Brierley guide says there will be a short incline to Portillo de las Cabras, the Pass of the Goats. For the first and probably only time, I am wishing for an incline as it will tell me we are almost there. Up and over and it is a gentle one thank Heavens. On the way down, on the outskirts of Los Arcos, there is a back garden with lots of little goats skipping around, so Chris stops to take a photo. Later on when I got home I looked at Katie's album on Facebook and she has taken the same shot. Me, I was just glad of the excuse to stop and rest for a few minutes. As we walk into town I am completely shattered. We pass by the first albergue with the intention of stopping at the municipal but just outside the next one, Casa de la Abuela, we meet an American lady and her husband. We had met them fleetingly in Estella and she tells us that all our friends are in this one. We are greeted by a Dutchman at reception. Apparently this albergue is run by a Dutch evangelical group. What a welcome. He has no lower bunks left but seeing a man who has obviously drained his tank he throws his arms around me, gives me a hug and grabs my rucksack and carries it up stairs for me. This was to be the only occasion on this first part of my Camino where I couldn't get a lower bunk. I hear an American accent offer to swap bunks with me, it's Mike again. We keep meeting. Apart from Mike and Gerry, Tom, the Korean girl from Dublin, Fernandez from Brazil and Maurice from Malta are all here. Our host recommends a restaurant down in the town so off we go. There is some difficulty translating the menu and eventually the waitress points at one item and moos like a cow, points at the other and flaps her arms like a chicken. I took the beef. A short while later, Tom and a few others join us and we recount the story about the waitress. When she comes to take their order they all either flap or moo and I still wonder how she felt about that. For dessert I pick what I think is yoghurt, it's a big unpeeled orange. Not what I had expected but it will make a nice lunch tomorrow. Back to the albergue and once again it is time for bed. I have done my first Brierley day as we have come to call them. Can I do another tomorrow all the way to Logroño, 28.6km? I doubt it very much

Buenos Noches y Buen Camino

Los Arcos to Viana

Day Six, Friday, 22nd March

Today we have an early start as the weather forecast is for a very sunny and hot day so we must get as far as we can before it gets too warm for walking. The first 5km is fairly flat. Although we were about first on the road, it isn't long before other peregrinos start to pass us. The American lady and her Spanish husband go by quickly then along comes Maurice from Malta who is, in his own words, taking it easy. If that's taking it easy he must be faster than '*The Flash*' when he is really moving. Eventually we resume our normal place for the day '*Tail End Charlies*'. We never met up with Maurice or the American lady again.

The path now starts to rise to the town of Sansol. It sits on top of one side of a valley or canyon cut by the Rio San Pedro and on the other side of the valley atop the hill there is Torres del Rio. It's a steep climb up to Sansol then a steep drop to the river followed immediately by another steep climb up the other side to Torres del Rio. It's a good place to stop for a bite of lunch. For anyone who still has enough in their tank when they reached Los Arcos, the extra 8km or so to the albergue in Torres del Rio would be well worth it. It is modern and clean, with its own swimming pool and bar. I would have loved to have stopped here.

Now the climb gets really tough, especially as the sun has come out and it is very hot. At the top we decide to stop and have something to eat. We had some snacks, the orange from last night and a chorizo sausage that we had bought in Torres del Rio. It's something new to us but it turns out to be very tasty and I will buy some more of it in the days ahead. As we sit enjoying a simple picnic in the sun on top of a mountain a

[40]

Frenchman arrives who is walking on his own and he stops to chat for a while before he is on his way. Before we move on, Chris suggests I phone Margaret. I start to tell her about our adventures and she listens, and then tells me that she is snowed in. It started to snow the day we left and has continued ever since. There is two feet of snow in the back garden but out the front it has drifted much deeper and the cars are almost covered. It has been the worst snow since 1963 and I am not at home to help out. I feel kind of useless at this moment in our Camino but there is nothing I can do but walk on. It's a steep descent to the Rio Cornava but then a fairly level walk at times criss crossing the N-111 all the way to the next town, Viana.

Viana is a medieval town, changed little over the centuries. Like most towns in old Europe, it was built on top of a hill for defensive purposes in the lawless days of the 15th Century. Because it's on a hill it can be seen from a long way off but when you are tired, it seems like it never gets any closer. The path now runs parallel to the N-111 road, the main road to Logroño. It has been a lovely day, a day for sun hats, sun cream, shorts and walking in our shirt sleeves but, on the horizon and moving quickly our way, are some really black clouds. A stop at a roadside picnic table is called for as we can actually see the rain falling in the distance. Once the waterproof jackets are on, it's a brisk walk now to get to town before the rain. We didn't make it and the skies opened and it rained like there was no tomorrow and a strong wind turned the rain horizontal. As we trudge into town wet and miserable we come across an albergue not mentioned in the Brierley guide book, Albergue Izar. In we go as it's too wet to try finding anywhere else. The place is empty except for the Frenchman we had met earlier. He is making pasta and invites us to join him but we choose to go out for a meal, a mistake as it turns out. It is Friday night and they are getting ready for Holy Week, Sunday being Palm Sunday. In Spain they call it Semana Santa and it's a real occasion for them and a national Holiday. They take the week up to Easter Sunday whereas we take the week after Easter Sunday. I think they have the better idea as the whole week was a great festival and a great time to be on the Camino. But I digress. Because they have just started their holiday, everyone is in party mode so the bars are not catering for food until much later by which time the albergue doors will be closed. Our first visit to a supermarket albeit a small one provides us with bread, butter, tuna and chocolate. Tuna toasties back in the albergue are on the menu. When we get back, the hospitalero has finished our washing for us and hung it out to dry. That was very nice of her. Our bellies are full and she has told us there will be breakfast included in the price and arranges a time to open up in the morning. I don't know why this albergue is not mentioned by Mr Brierley in his book but it should be. I could recommend it to anyone. So that is it for another day

Buenos Noches y Buen Camino

Viana to Logroño

Day Seven, Saturday, 23rd March

As we were about to leave Viana the hospitalero advised us not to fill our water bottles from the town mains. We would find out later what she meant as some of the town water although safe to drink, tastes really foul. Just outside of town we met Sarah and Kathleen coming towards us. Apparently they left without their walking poles and were hoping to get back into the albergue, which was now closed, to retrieve them. We would meet them one more time on our journey.

The trail now turns into a tunnel under the N-111. At the far end someone has painted a large scallop shell with the words Buen Camino beneath. We have seen lots of graffiti along the way but this is special.

We are now tramping through fields again and every other one seems to be a vineyard but as I said before, at this time of year they look like row after row of dead stumps. Quite ugly compared to what they will look like in a few months.

We hear a call from behind and turn round to see Mike and Gerry. How do we keep getting ahead of them? They had stopped in the municipal albergue in Viana but as usual Gerry was in no hurry to get out of his bed so we have made it most of the way to Logroño before they caught up. This time however I came to regret seeing them again. Mike has a bad cold and before long I will have it too. This sadly though is the last time we will meet. I had really grown to like these two guys. I just wish I had thought to ask them their surnames and got some contact details. I wonder did they make it to Santiago, I am sure they did.

As we approach the border with La Rioja, Mike and Gerry have gone on as I am walking quite slowly today but we are caught up by a Dutchman and his daughter. We walk together for some time until we come to a wayside stall. This stall is run by an old woman called Felisa. She has been here since she was a child helping her aunt also called Felisa. I guess between them they have been sitting here for the best part of one hundred years. Felisa has a young girl with her and I wonder will she in her turn take over the stall and keep it going into her old age. Felisa will stamp your credentials for you and I believe your camino is not complete without this special stamp. Our Dutch friends however don't seem to know about this stall and don't get their Sello. It's free but a donativo seems fair so we give her €5 each and she wishes us a Buen Camino. In fact, everyone we meet along the way greets us just the same, makes us feel good to hear it.

As we enter Logroño there is a stunning water feature beside the river and a little girl, who has just made her first communion, is having her picture taken. As we watch, we are approached by what looks like another peregrino complete with rucksack, hiking clothes and boots. He tells us he is German and has fallen on hard times. He pulls an old chewed up bank card from his wallet and says the machine chewed it up so he can't get any money. There is a free albergue in town that he points us to but says the f*****g priest won't let him stay in it. He is trying to find some German pilgrims he got separated from to borrow some money to get to the German consul in Vigo where he can pick up some money being transferred from home. I know in my heart that it's a scam and he is spinning us a yarn but just in case, in the most unlikely scenario he is telling the truth, I give him €10. Chris tells me that I have been conned and I know he is right, but just in case!!!

It's only been a 10km hike today so we decide to rest up in Logroño. As it's not quite lunch time, we have loads of time to relax, get a meal and explore the town. We have dropped our bags in the municipal albergue and are now scouting around for a place to eat. After looking at a few places we decide on a restaurant in the town square opposite the Cathedral. Now, as I said before, I am not one for going abroad and then looking for Irish pubs and drinks, but this place has Murphy's Red which is very similar to my favourite that I got back in Trabolgan, Co

Cork, Beamish Red. So good I go back later for another. It's a pity the two red ales I like are export only and not available in Ireland.

As today is the eve of Palm Sunday, the town is getting ready for one of the biggest days of the year and the floats of Jesus arriving in Jerusalem are being wheeled out of storage and into the Cathedral just outside the window we are sitting at, so I got some good photos.

After we have finished lunch, it's off to explore the city. Like most of the big cities along the Camino, it is a mix of the old and the modern. One minute you are walking along medieval streets, you turn a corner and you are in a modern city. It is quite amazing. We eventually make our way back to the albergue to see the dreaded sign on the door, 'Completo'. It's the first time I have seen it and I hope it's the last. A bus load of youngsters has arrived from Ireland and they have been allowed to stay in the albergue. Peregrinos who have walked hundreds of kilometres are being turned away. I am sorry, but this is just not right. These kids should have been put up in a hostel or hotel as they are not peregrinos as such. They get dropped by bus, walk a few miles next day and then get picked up again and taken to the next stop. I got no problem with how they do it and in fact we walked some way with them the next day, they just should not be taking up albergue places needed by very tired walkers.

As tomorrow is Palm Sunday we feel like we really should find a Mass somewhere. Problem is that the only times we can find clash with the times the restaurants are open for evening meals. As luck would have it a young couple are getting married

[45]

in a church just round the corner from the albergue at 6pm. A bit cheeky I know, but we slip in the back and attend their wedding Mass. Our duty done we slip out just before Mass ends so we don't get in the way. We got a few funny looks from some guests but what the heck, any port in a storm as they say. I hope we did not ruin any wedding photos.

Back in the albergue I have time to write up my journal. It has been a bit rushed this last couple of days as I have been so tired but today has been very relaxing. I have time to sit and think tonight. I am very worried about Margaret and Sarah with all that snow, no electricity and no heating. I am annoyed at our kids. Do they not realise their Mammy is in dire straits at the minute just because the snow is not as bad where they are? I am in Spain and I can see the news about the north of Ireland and the six to ten feet walls of snow along the roads. I just get so angry because it seems nobody cares about the trouble Margaret is in. I know she couldn't read it and probably never will but I write in my journal 'Margaret, I love you so much and miss you lots xxxxx'. I am beginning to realise that my Way, my Camino, is back home to Ireland to the wife who loves me even though sometimes, she pretends she doesn't. She has had a hard life caring for me and our seven children. She deserves a compostela more than I ever will.

Buenos Noches y Buen Camino

Logroño to Navarette

Day Eight, Palm Sunday, 24th March

This morning must be the coldest morning we have had so far. I am tired and hungry and feel so miserable that I just want to go home; I really don't want to do this anymore. The walk through Logroño is boring but well way marked. All along the route there are scallop shells embedded in the footpaths. As we make our way out of town into parkland we see a familiar face coming towards us. It's Amanda from Australia. We met her and her friend Robin back on Perdón. Robin was here to go all the way but Amanda was time limited and her time was now up. She had walked some way out of town with Robin to complete 100 miles and was now heading back to town to get a bus and go home. I hope she had a pleasant journey.

As we walk along the park pathways lots of joggers are passing us by. Today is Palm Sunday and the Spanish holiday of Semana Santa is well and truly started. We are passed by a Dutch guy who then stops just ahead for a smoke. I don't think it was a regular cigarette he was smoking, smelt funny, but right now I don't care. I am starting to get on Christopher's nerves as I moan and complain. I have been tired, I have been completely exhausted, I have been in a lot of pain but this is the first time I have been ready to give in to despair. Maybe some food will help so we stop at a park bench and I have some dry bread with chorizo sausage for breakfast. Not bad actually. Chris keeps telling me there is a good café ahead but it seems to be always round the next corner. At last we come to the lake he was talking about, La Grajera. All along the bank there are dozens of people fishing but I don't care about them, ahead I can see the café.

Our fear that the Café Cabaña Tio Juarvi, would be closed because it was a public holiday are unfounded so in we go for coffee and snacks. Sitting outside is a Dutch guy we had previously met briefly, called Tierde. Just then, a little red

 squirrel fearlessly approaches us and climbs up onto my backpack that I had carelessly dropped in the middle of the café forecourt. Thankfully it climbs down and runs off to meet somebody else. That back pack is heavy enough

without having to carry a passenger. It's amazing how a good café con leche can lift the miseries and bring the jokes out. The sun is well up now and it is pleasantly warm, the coffee is hot and the company is good. At last all seems right with the world and when Tierde suggests another cup of coffee we don't need to be asked twice. An hour ago I wanted to quit now that's all gone. The Camino does provide. That is the popular saying, but it is God that provides and he certainly is providing for me and, what do you know, I *am* getting religious.

Sitting here all day seems an attractive proposition but at last it is time to move on. The three of us walk along for a short distance then Tierde says he wants to push on ahead. He had problems that brought him on the Camino and he wanted to walk alone and sort out his life in his head. I hope he found the peace he was looking for, we never met him again.

We are now faced with a fairly steep climb up to Alto Grajera. I don't like hills at the best of times but this one is very steep. It's only about 150 metres in height but it rises in about 3km. I have decided that I will not greet other pilgrims with the usual 'Hola, Buen Camino' anymore. I will use the English Hello so that anyone passing will know we are English speakers. It works a treat. A petite lady passes us by and stops when she hears 'Hello'. She is Elizabeth from Australia. She has made the journey here alone and has been relying on meeting people along the way and although she is fitter and faster than me she slows her pace to walk with us.

As we pass the summit the trail joins the road to Navarette and at this point some of the kids who packed out the albergue last night go bye and on down the road. As we are walking along chatting with Elizabeth we aimlessly follow them until we hear a farmer call us. We were just about to miss the turn off where the trail goes back onto farmland paths. I suppose the kids made it to their pick up point as road and path go to the same place. The walking has been tough and it's really quite warm now so we are glad to stop at San Juan de Acre ruins, the site of a medieval monastery founded in the 12th century to look after peregrinos. Just past it is a large bodega specialising in guess what, Rioja, so another photo stop. At last we trudge into Navarette. It's only been about 12km but it's so hot I think that we have done enough for today. We stop at a little café for lunch and for me, that's a cold beer and an enormous bocadillo with a massive tortilla as filling. Lovely. By the way, never go into a bar in Spain and ask for a San Miguel pronounced Migwell. Its Meegel. The barmaid did not have a clue what I was asking for until another customer, a local, explained it.

Chris suggests we go and sit in front of the albergue until it opens in case the bus load of kids arrive and fill it up before we can get in. Besides, it is in what I can only describe as a covered walkway or arcade well shaded from the midday sun. Word quickly spreads that Mass is getting out and a festival is about to start. In the plaza in front of the church there are bands, dressed in monastic style robes, playing and all the children are dressed in what looks like their first communion finery. They have all been given branches of palm with sweets and gifts attached and the local bar is doing a roaring trade. This is the kind of festival we should have in Ireland instead of thinking of Palm Sunday as the day that the gospel goes on forever. Later in the day, I went for a walk and visited the church. As I sat in front of the statue of Our Lady, I began to cry. I didn't know why then, and still don't know but there was something about that church, that statue and Palm Sunday that made me emotional. Maybe I am starting to get the spiritual side of the Camino but it is a strange and new emotion for me.

The albergue is now opened so in we go and get settled for the day. Rick, whom we met in Monjardín, arrives and we have our first meeting with the gentle giant from Galway, Big Phil. I heard some weeks later that even with all the problems he had with his feet, he made it to Santiago. He deserved a medal along with his compostela. Phil in true Irish fashion decides we all need to go to the bar for a drink. I don't need my arm twisting so off we go, just him and me. It's amazing how a guy I have met for the first time just an hour ago is now my drinking buddy. It's easy to make friends on the Camino. As we finish our drink I hear a Texan drawl behind me and Big Jim joins us at the bar. He is staying in a hotel further into town.

We are now planted at the bar for the rest of the afternoon so in true Spanish tradition the barman brings us some tapas. One of the waitresses asks where we are from and corrects my pronunciation when I say '*soy Irlandés*'. The other waitress says something I can't understand and the first one says she has said in Basque '*you are Irish? Oh well, nobody is perfect*' and everyone laughs at my expense, even me. Time to go and we all agree to meet up here for dinner later which we do. We are joined for the meal by Elizabeth, K1 and K2, and a cyclist, Peter from Bantry. That is a meal I will remember for as long as I live. It was an evening of great food, good wine and fantastic company. As we say in Ireland, you can't beat the craic.

Tonight I hear someone who can snore more than me. Big Phil, you could snore for Ireland

We have been walking now for a full week

Buenos Noches y Buen Camino

Navarette to Nájera

Day Nine, Monday, 25th March

It's a bit of a tough walk today but I have had tougher in the last seven days. Chris has walked on ahead with Rick and I have been walking with Phil and Peter who has decided to enjoy the company and push his bike for a while. However, as usual, I am slower than everyone else so eventually I am walking on my own for the first time. It gives me time to think and my thoughts are of Margaret stuck at home in all that snow. What on earth possessed me to leave her and come on this pointless walk? It does seem to be pointless at the minute as I am still unsure of my reasons for doing it. Is it spiritual, is it bravado or is it just a reawakening of the wander lust I had as a child and young man? If I can't answer this question then what is the point in being here instead of with my wife at home. I knew I loved her but now I am beginning to realise just how much. God but I miss her.

Eventually I caught up with Chris and Rick. Not that I started walking faster, no, Rick had stopped for a cigarette. After we had rested at a point where the road crosses the camino, Rick explains that he wants to go on alone. He has told Chris about some issues he has and feels that he can only resolve them alone. As he walks off ahead of us into the distance, little did we know that we would never meet him again. I hope he had a successful camino and was able to, with the grace of God, work out his problems.

It seems that we are becoming famous along the way. Everyone appears to have heard of the father and son from Ireland, 'Padre y Niño'. A Canadian couple speak to us as they pass us by and ask if we are the ones from Ireland. After we confirm it they head of at quite a pace. The girl is well weighed down with camera equipment and I wish I could have brought mine but I have more to carry than I need already. I notice that the Canadians have stopped up ahead and the girl has gone way off to the right into a field with her camera. Apparently she is writing a book and was taking pictures of us to include in it. Says we are getting a section of our own. Who knows, maybe we will see our names in another book on the Camino someday.

Along the way we came across a beehive style building, something akin to the beehives in Kerry back in Ireland. The path is fairly level at this stage and there are quite a few wild flowers growing at the side of the path. After the steep climbs of earlier in the day this is a reasonably easy bit of walking and we can spare the time to take a few pictures

It is raining now. The first persistent rain since we landed in Spain. I have developed a cold, thanks Mike, the one time I would have preferred not to meet you as we walked into Logroño a few days ago. Unfortunately, the day I caught Mike's cold was to be the last time we ever met. I would love to know how they got on.

As we entered the town of Nájera, who should we meet but the German guy who was scrounging off pilgrims outside Logroño. He is still passing himself off as a pilgrim and using the same hard luck story. As he approached us we let him know we had already met him before and asked how he was getting on conning money to get to Vigo. In German, he said something that was obviously not very nice. It gave us a laugh in this awful rain.

The first albergue we came to was only taking pilgrims who had booked in advance so we headed along the river to the municipal. On the way, who should come out of a shop but Big Phil? He had already booked in. Bit of a strange place. The bunks were all laid out in twos, meaning that effectively, the person in the next bunk was sharing a bed with me. An unusual layout but I suppose it means they can accommodate more pilgrims. It's not a money making thing by the way. This albergue was donativo (voluntary donation). Before we can go in however I get another Spanish lesson. The little old lady volunteer hospitalera won't let me go until I say Nájera correctly with the emphasis on the accented á. They say you learn something new every day.

Along the approaches to Nájera were posters about a bar with menu de peregrino, but it was closed and stayed closed. Also as you approach Nájera, painted on a factory wall is a poem

> 'The force that drives me
>
> The force that draws me
>
> I am unable to explain
>
> Only He above knows'

We did not actually see this poem but it is mentioned in a CTS Camino booklet by David Baldwin.

Tonight we learned about '*cocino abierto*'. The kitchens along the way opened around 7pm to 8pm but here in Nájera it was 8 at the earliest. We were too hungry to wait that long but what could we do. Luckily we found a bar where we could get something to eat. Not a three course pilgrim meal but substantial enough to fill our bellies. The owner told us he opened early for breakfast (desayuno) and gave us a flyer to pass around. This guy was so friendly we determined to return in the morning for our early morning coffee and we would tell others about him.

For now though, it is time to settle down for the night and reflect on the coming day. Because I am so slow we have fallen behind schedule and we need to get to Burgos to arrange flights home for Chris on Holy Thursday and get him on a bus for Madrid airport. There is nothing for it but to take a bus from here in the morning. The estacion de autobus is just on the other side of the river and as far as I know there is a bus at eleven. I am going to miss my son. He has been marvellous and I honestly doubt I would have gotten this far without him. Oh well, we shall see what tomorrow brings. Once again it is time to call it a day and get some sleep

Buenos noches y buen camino

Najera to Burgos

Day 10, Tuesday, 26th March

As we are taking a bus to Burgos this morning we leave the albergue quite late. The same little old lady from last night is showing her stricter side as she urges and pushes the last stragglers out of the door by 8am. We also meet the Canadians who took our photos yesterday and they ask for our e-mail addresses so that they can send us copies of the photos but unfortunately, we never heard from them again.

We will miss out the stages to Santa Domingo de la Calzada, to Belorado and San Juan de Ortega unfortunately but we are way behind schedule. We avoid some very mountainous terrain especially from Belorado to San Juan de Ortega but it's not because I don't do mountains well. Chris has to fly out of Madrid on Thursday and I want to treat him to a rest day in a hotel before he goes. Unfortunately we will also miss out on visiting Atapuerca, the archaeological site where the earliest human remains in Europe have been discovered dating back 1,000,000 years. The caves were declared a UNESCO world heritage site in 2000.

The estacion de autobus is just across the river from the albergue but we have to pass the restaurant where we got such a good meal last night. I have passed on the details to other pilgrims which was a bit of a mistake. By the time we get there, Big Phil with us, it is full of the people we sent but we managed to get a seat and a breakfast. A bit more cramped than we had hoped for but it was a good start to the day. As we made to leave after paying our bill, the owner called us back. The camino is out the back door he explains. We hadn't the heart to tell him we were going for a bus so we went out the back and made our way through the back streets to the bridge over the river. Phil has decided that until his foot heals he will take buses to the various stages so that he gets all the sellos between here and Burgos. The bus station is just a waiting room at the side of the kerb and as we wait, we crack jokes about cheating; there are some purist pilgrims who would frown upon us for getting the bus. Although I had been told there was a bus at 11am I spot a sign on the bus waiting at the stop that says Burgos. A quick sprint out to speak to the driver confirms that this is the bus we want but Phil says he will wait for the next as he is not sure if this one stops at Santa Domingo. As we board the bus Phil pulls out his camera and says he will show the photos to everyone on the camino to prove we cheated and even though he is in agony with his feet he runs after the bus taking pictures as we wave out the window. I fear we have seen the last of him which is a pity as once again I have not thought of getting his surname.

At the next stop Sarah and Kathleen from Canada board the bus. I am almost certain they spotted us sitting down the back and rather sheepishly they take seats at the front. Eventually we pull into the estacion in Burgos and speak to the Canadians as we get off. A middle aged American couple are also on the bus. We have never met them before so as Sarah and Kathleen leave the station we stop for a chat. About fifteen minutes later the Canadians come back in and are somewhat embarrassed to see we are still there. They are carrying on to Leon by bus and didn't like to admit it. The camino is a very personal journey and it is no-one's privilege to say that their way is the right way so if a pilgrim needs to take a bus or train it is their decision and no-one has the right to criticise, certainly not me as later events will prove.

Instead of waiting until mañana we decide to get a ticket for Madrid now. As fate would have it another good decision. There are only three seats left on the bus. Once again, the angels are looking after us, or is it my son Paul. Each time any of our kids has gone travelling I have asked our son in heaven to be their guardian angel. This is his second camino as I asked him to look after Chris last year and I have asked him to come with us and watch over us this year. He is doing it well because everything that appeared at the time to be wrong turned out right in the end.

As we left the station, we turned left instead of right. Chris was throwing a bit of a tantrum because the ticket machine was not working properly so he stormed out the front door without paying attention to anything. The result was that we became hopelessly lost. Eventually I asked a woman '¿donde esta el rio?' I don't know if that is the correct way to ask 'where is the river' but she understood and pointed us in the right direction. At the river we realised just how far out of our way we had walked. We were way up past the bridge with the statue of El Cid and it was the next bridge past that where we should have been. Burgos was by the way, the birth place of Count Rodrigo Díaz de Vivar better known as El Cid.

Chris has now regained his composure so we stop to take some pictures of the statue. I must point out that El Cid looks nothing like Charlton Heston in the movie. The next bridge down is Arco y Puente de Santa Maria, that is, the arch and bridge of Santa Maria. As you cross the bridge there is a promenade of Spanish plane trees going left and right and straight ahead is the arch leading into Plaza Santa Maria wherein is the cathedral. The promenades by the way were planted by the Napoleonic authorities when they occupied Burgos during Napoleon's invasion of Spain. Behind the Cathedral is the association albergue Casa Del Cubo. It has just opened its doors at 1pm so we get a good bed at the end of the dorm. Each dorm is partitioned into sets of four bunks sleeping eight people. As we got the partition at the end there were only two bunks so we would only have to share with two other people. One who got in just before us is a girl from Barcelona who seems to know her way about this town. She is heading off to the Museum of Human History but tells us that at a certain time pilgrims can get into the cathedral museum for free. Before we do anything though I feel I should ring Margaret rather than an impersonal text. She has been out in the snow. She had to get the bus to the doctors and thought she just might do some shopping while she was out. She forgot that she would have a bit of a walk carrying shopping bags. At this time, none of our kids have contacted her to see if she needs anything. Only Nicola has contacted her and has asked for shore leave while her ship is in dry dock, so that she can come home to help her Mum.

I have booked a room in the Meson El Cid hotel right in front of the Cathedral and the room will be ready at noon. As we must be out of the albergue by eight, we will have four hours to kill but that's tomorrow's problem. Just off the plaza in Lain Calvo we found a little restaurant and got a good meal. However their credit card machines were not working so I had to use the last €30 we had in cash. Now we shall see how these prepaid credit cards work in an atm, fortunately, no problem. After our meal we stepped out into the street and bumped into Cecilia whom we had met in Mañeru. She was looking for somewhere good to eat so we recommended the place we had just left. I don't know if she went in or not but it was the last time I seen her. Hope she made it to Santiago.

Back in the albergue it is time for some running repairs. The middle finger on my right hand has become infected. It has been hurting me since we left home and the pressure on it from the walking poles has stopped it from healing. My whiskey, which I brought purely for medicinal purposes of course, comes in handy. I use it to sterilize a needle and wash my finger before piercing the site of the infection. The amount of puss coming out surprises me. Once it is washed again and dressed I think I deserve a little mouthful of said whiskey. Purely medicinal, you understand.

The cathedral has now opened its doors to the peregrinos so off we go. First we get the cathedral Sello then go for a wander around the massive interior. It is very impressive and we get loads of photos including one of a painting of El Cid. Now this

looks a bit more like Mr Heston, not a lot mind you, but more so than the wildman look of the statue. We finish the afternoon with a snack in the Black Book, an Irish bar. That will keep us going until dinner then an early night.

Buenos noches y buen camino

Rest Day In Burgos

Day Eleven, Wednesday, 17th March (Spy Wednesday)

Not a very nice morning. It is raining fairly heavily so we wander about looking for somewhere to shelter until the hotel room is ready. We reckon there must be a MacDonald's where we can sit over a burger for a while and enjoy their free wi-fi. Well, guess what, there is not a single fast food joint in Burgos. I found out later that there is one in an out of town shopping centre but none in the city. We might as well try the hotel early. As we head back towards the hotel, I spot a statue of someone wearing a helmet and with his right arm pointing up. From behind I assume, since Burgos was his headquarters, that it is Franco giving a fascist salute. It is only of a policeman however, directing traffic so Chris high fives it.

If the room is not ready we can buy a drink and sit in the bar for an hour or two, but as luck would have it, the room is ready. After a little rest, we repack our rucksacks. Chris is taking home some of my surplus belongings and my backpack and leaving his for me. He has lovingly christened his pack Matilda. Don't know why but, Matilda it is.

So that I will know where I am going in the morning we take a walk along the camino out of the town centre. This is a practice I will adopt later so that in the dark mornings I won't get lost.

It's quite an unspectacular day with just a little bit of shopping for souvenirs that Chris can bring home with him. As night approaches, there are still a few showers about so we try to

[58]

stay close to the hotel when we go in search of food. As we enjoy our meal, Tom from Kilkenny and the Korean girl turn up and join us for dinner. The girl tells us that she dropped out of university in Dublin to come on the Camino and reckons that when she returns to Ireland she will be deported as she was in the country on a student visa and she is not a student any longer. I hope she got to Santiago and got to stay in Ireland. When Tom hears that Chris is going home tomorrow he gives me his mobile number in case I get into any difficulties. He is a good lad this boy from Kilkenny. I didn't need his number which I still have, but I never met him again.

I am not looking forward to the morning. I am really afraid of carrying on alone. I know they say you never walk alone on the Camino but I still feel very apprehensive. I need someone to walk with and Chris won't be here anymore. I know that Jesus and my guardian angel are with me but as I am one of those who fit into the category of, 'ye of little faith', I need someone of flesh and blood that I can see and talk too. Tomorrow I will head for the famous Meseta and Hornillos del Camino. It will be Holy Thursday, the day of the Last Supper and the Agony in the Garden and tonight I am going through my own agony after having my last supper with Chris and Tom. Semana Santa is fast coming to an end

Buenos noches y buen camino

Burgos to Hornillos (alone, or am I)

Day Twelve, Thursday, 28th March (Holy Thursday)

It's still dark and the hotel restaurant has not yet opened for breakfast but I can't wait any longer. If I don't get on the road soon, I will not go on alone and will probably try to book a plane ticket home with Chris. I pay the night assistant for our stay in the hotel and after a few tears and hugs, I send Chris back to the room and I plunge into the dark of a sleeping city. Just up the road there is a fuenta (fountain) where I can fill my water bottles before setting out for my first stop of the day about 12km further on at Tarjados. The trail is long and flat with nothing much to see except for a long orange building that turns out to be a state penitentiary or gaol to us Irish. As I have already said, Burgos was Franco's headquarters during the civil war and I wonder how many of his opponents went into that prison never to be seen again. In the 50s, thousands of political prisoners were transported from all over Spain to Valencia and there murdered by Franco firing squads. It has been estimated that somewhere in the region of 50,000 people are buried in mass graves that became rubbish dumps around that city.

By the time I reach Villabilla the rain has started and I am feeling even more miserable than I did when I left Chris. Doubts are entering my mind about this whole foolish adventure. What the hell am I doing wandering across northern Spain wet cold and miserable? Why did I come on this camino I keep asking myself but I never get a satisfactory answer. I want so much to go home to be with Margaret. I am starting to realise just how much I love her, miss her and need her. It is killing me being away from her knowing she is stuck in the house in such bad weather. I have told Chris to text me when he gets home if things are bad enough that I should also come home. He may be pre occupied though because he doesn't know that his girlfriend from Cork will be waiting at Dublin airport. I keep wondering if maybe I should have told him but it's too late now.

The trail crosses a road and I very nearly take a wrong turning but someone is looking after me as I will find many times in the future and I get pushed by what I believe is a divine hand in the right direction. I started the day by praying saying my morning offertory, the prayer to my guardian angel and a prayer to Our Lady of the Miraculous Medal. These are the only formal prayers I will say at any time on the camino. I find it better to talk to Jesus as if he was another pilgrim walking beside me. No thee and thou or dear lords. More like as we say in Belfast 'bout ye' how you doin and any chance of a wee push here. I ask for help just as I would from a friend because he is my friend, least I hope he is. If I were him, I wouldn't bother with a sinner like me. Maybe that's why I am here. The germ of an idea is forming that maybe its penance for my past life and I offer my suffering up for the souls in purgatory. I am definitely getting religious. I am finding a faith I have not experienced since I was a kid. Maybe it is true; the Camino changes the hiker into a pilgrim.

A small SUV approaches along the trail and the driver is handing out leaflets for a bar/café in Tarjados so I think I must be pretty close, so close I can almost smell the café con leche. Well, it's not as close as I hoped and I am still walking 30 minutes later but I am so tired that it feels like hours but at last I walk into town and quickly find that café. A coffee and a tortilla and I am feeling refreshed but my foot is hurting so I decide to sit down under the awning outside and get my boot off. While I am applying Vaseline to my foot another pilgrim stops to ask if this is the way to Rabe de las Calzados. He is limping very badly but even though I suggest he stops for a rest he insists on pushing on. Eventually, having finished tending to my feet I get back on the road again. I have found along the way that when my feet start to feel a bit hot and painful, getting them out in the open air and smearing them with Vaseline really helps. Wish I had brought the balm specially made for pilgrims with me. Chris had bought it last year but insisted we did not need it and it was just extra weight. Well, he is not right about everything camino related, this time he was wrong but too late finding out now.

As I leave the town I come across the limping pilgrim and I slow down to talk to him. Imagine me slowing down for anyone; it's usually the other way round. His name is Carlos and he is from Costa Rica. He slipped and fell in the snow back at Roncesvalles and cracked his knee on a rock that was just below the surface. He has been hobbling all the way ever since. This guy has walked further than me, took no buses, and on a badly damaged knee and I am complaining. He has put me to shame.

I had planned to stop at Rabe and so had Carlos. When we get there however, the albergue is not yet opened so he sits by the door and I sit on a park bench on the other side of the plaza and I watch him take off the heavy bandage and massage his knee. He eventually rises and tells me he is not going to wait

[61]

for the albergue to open and is going to push on. Should I go with him or sit here like a wimp waiting for a bed. The answer is 'Ultreya', onwards.

As we climb up onto the Meseta I start to feel really tired again and even Carlos is walking faster than me. We hear the tinkling of bells and an Austrian girl with bells attached to her DIY bordon passes by with a cheery greeting and wave. What she has to be cheery about in this drizzle, I don't know. At last the rain stops so we stop for some refreshment and Carlos shares an orange with me. He has told me his story and I have told him mine but his story is between him and me and not for this journal. On we go a few more steps around a bend and there is the Austrian girl in a little shelter just off the trail having her lunch. Had I looked closer at my guide I would have seen the picnic table symbol and avoided sitting on a rock for lunch.

Still the trail continues to rise. God will it ever end I ask and just at that we come over a crest and we are at the top, Alto Meseta, 950m above sea level. It felt more like Everest than the Cave Hill back home. We can see the downward slope now. A lot steeper going down than up and Carlos is really struggling on this stretch but I still feel uneasy about leaving him and have done so since we first joined up at Tarjados. Half way down the hill, his face contorted with pain he says in his broken English "Terry, this is my Compostela". I take that to mean he is going to finish here and go no further but I feel it is best not

to speak about it so we carry on in mostly silence to the outskirts of Hornillos. The approach to the town is flooded on both sides and I later find out that a few days after I had passed by, the road was also flooded and a helpful farmer was ferrying pilgrims into town in the bucket of his digger.

At the albergue we cannot find the hospitalera and someone tells us she owns the bar at the bottom of the plaza and we will find her there. The place is chaotic, pilgrims everywhere looking for bar service, others wanting restaurant service and us wanting a bed. An English girl, Rowena, whom we had met briefly back in Rabe tries to speak on our behalf to hear the dreaded word 'completo'. However Rowena says there are still two beds in her dorm and we should just go and take them which we do before heading back to the bar for food. There we find that the hospitalero meant the restaurant at the back was full up, not the albergue. At last a table is ready and Carlos and I share a fine meal during which the hospitalera takes our pilgrim passports and explains via Carlos that she will be stamping them in the basement of the albergue later.

Rowena announces that she has decided not to stay and is moving on with someone called Robin who has just arrived. Could it be Robin from Australia who was so kind to me back in Uterga on my first day walking? I dash into the plaza and it is indeed her. She has a new crew now as I call them, Rowena from England and Pat from Ireland and they are pushing on to the next stop. I don't know if she means San Bol or Hontanas but both are too far for me so after some catching up and hugs she sets off up the hill towards the second part of the Meseta. I never saw her again. I hope she made it all the way.

As its Holy Thursday, there is a misa (mass) in the church attached to the albergue so Carlos and I decide to attend as does almost every other pilgrim in town. During the mass when we offer each other a sign of peace, Carlos crosses the aisle and throws his arms around me with tears in his eyes. I know I will not see this man again and I also know that meeting him was not by chance. The Lord sent him to help me on my way. Not the last time he will do this in my hour of need. He has got me through a Brierly day, 22km over rough terrain in miserable weather by sending this man to be my companion when I needed one so badly. Once again I repeat, you never walk alone on the Camino.

One person that I must not forget was the girl from Iran/Persia/England/Spain that I met at the bar. I don't know her name. She was a very soft spoken young woman who prefers to say she came from Persia rather than Iran. Her parents brought her to London as a child where she grew up but now lives in Malaga on the Mediterranean coast. I will meet her again in unusual circumstances but for now its

Buenos Noches y Buen Camino

Hornillos to Castrojeriz

Day Thirteen, Friday, 29th March   (Good Friday)

After an early breakfast with a Spanish family I met briefly last night, I stepped out into the dark and started the climb up to the second part of the Meseta. There is a bitter wind, very cold but at least it's dry. Carlos is still on my mind and I feel sorry to have left him behind. I wonder should I have waited for him to rise and say goodbye properly. I enjoyed his company yesterday and without it I probably would not have made it as far as Hornillos. I hope everything works out for him. This was probably his one and only chance to walk the Camino.

The climb is tough but I am refreshed after a good night's sleep so I don't tire as much as I usually do on hills. Half way up, the Spanish family pass me. The Spanish, unlike us in Ireland, have their Easter break during Semana Santa (Holy Week) whereas we have ours after Easter. Many Spaniards walk part of the Camino at this time and that is what this family is doing. They will finish either tomorrow or Easter Sunday, and then make their way home ready for work on Monday.

The terrain now dips into a river valley at the Rio San Bol. There is a famous albergue just off the camino at this point but I am not thinking of stopping after just 5km. I climb the short hill up the other side of the valley in fairly good spirits. The going has not been as tough as I thought but that is all about to change dramatically. I am travelling through cultivated fields and the trail has been shared with farm vehicles. The mud has been churned up something fierce and I am finding it very difficult to pick my way through it and eventually it becomes so bad there is no way through it. There are just no dry spots left so there is no choice but to just plough on into it. It clings to my boots and with each step it pulls more energy from my muscles. I spot some people in the distance who have climbed up onto the cultivated field so I think I will try it. This is as bad if not worse than the mud. The loose rich soil sticks and doesn't fall of like the mud. My boots look twice the size and feel twice as heavy. This is starting to really drain me, more so than any hill has done up to now. At last there is a little relief where the trail crosses the road between Iglesias and Villandiego and I can sit down on a roadside rock to scrape the mud of my boots. Not really much point as I can see that the trail ahead is as bad as that behind. If I had but known, had I taken the road towards Villandiego, there is a turn off for Hontanas just a short distance away. There is only about another 2km of this left until the trail starts downhill but it may as well be 20. At this point I meet a lady who is guiding a blind man. She picks out the path and he holds on to her shoulder as they move along. They appear to be struggling as much as I am. Two girls, in their twenties I would guess, overtake us and stop to ask if we need any help as I am feeling and looking somewhat distressed. I choose to walk with just one pole this morning so I ask them to get my other pole of my pack as there is nowhere I can take it off and set down in this mud. After they have got my other pole they say they are off but will keep checking back at each bend to make sure myself and the blind man are ok. True to their word, I see them look back before disappearing round any bends in the trail. To look at the guide book you would think the trail was as straight as an arrow but there are some slight bends.

Hontanas is positioned on the slope down off the Meseta so it isn't visible until you are almost on top of it. It appears suddenly like a welcome beacon to the weary pilgrim. It is a steep slope down but dry, lovely beautiful dry soil. There is a little rest area on the edge of town with a fountain where I stop to fill my bottles and just past that, there is a little bar attached to a private albergue, El Puntido. It is full of pilgrims. I don't feel comfortable just walking in so I sit down at a table outside to clean as much mud as I can off my boots. As usual, leaving ones rucksack and walking poles outside is risk free. No-one will touch them. As I enter, the two girls that befriended me up on the Meseta call out to me. *"You made it, we will head on now, Buen Camino"*. They had waited to make sure I arrived safely. After a well-earned café con leche and a tortilla bocadillo, it is time to push on. Just down the street there is another albergue and it is open. I wonder, should I stay or not? As I walk on, I think I may be crazy but on I go. The bar owner has told us that the trail ahead is washed out and we should take the road. The girl I met in Hornillos from Persia/England/Spain is also heading out of town and just ahead is the blind man who has been joined by another blind man with a guide dog. At the last minute the girl and her companion decide to try the trail but I stick to the road. The blind group are pulling further away until I lose sight of them and then the rain comes on; heavy and persistent. I have gone too far to turn back to the albergue so on I go. The trail re-joins the road just before the ruins of San Anton and as I approach the junction the Persian girl comes out onto the road. She walks with me a little way and before leaving to catch up on her companion, gets my spare water

[65]

bottle from my pack and fills up the trusty bottle that hangs in a holster around my neck and then she is gone.

The albergue in the ruins is closed and won't be operational for a few weeks yet but the rain has stopped so it is a good spot to have a break. Some chocolate, mixed nuts and water. Refreshed, I resume my journey. At a little crossroad, a sporty sounding car comes out onto the road and the driver guns the engine and zooms of towards Castrojeriz. It feels like he was rubbing it in showing off in front of a weary pilgrim. To make matters worse, about ten minutes later he came back. That's how long it took him to get to my destination and back and it's going to take me at least another hour. I have been walking for a long time now. I started out before dawn and it's about 4pm now. That is approximately 10 hours walking through some pretty awful terrain. The rain has come back on and I am feeling really miserable now. So tired, I can barely put one foot in front of the other, even putting one pole in front of the other has become a chore as my arms are also feeling like lead. Matilda is pulling the back out of me and the pain is becoming unbearable. Again I start to question, what the hell am I doing here. Why on earth did I ever contemplate this insane journey at my age? I want to go home to Margaret. I keep myself going by thinking of the walk Jesus had to do on Good Friday. He had a cross to carry; all I have is a 10kilo back pack

Wouldn't you know it? There is a steep wee hill up into the town and I become unsure of my bearings. I haven't seen any signs for albergues or any yellow arrows either. Around a corner I come across a family parked at the side of the road in a blue people carrier. The mother has some English and directs me down a path to an albergue. It leads me into a caravan park and I remember reading that part of the main building is an albergue. As I approach the door a man comes out and shoos me away. This is a camp site not an albergue he tells me and points me up into the town. I don't know what he was playing at but it definitely is an albergue as I confirm later on the internet. At last I find a yellow arrow pointing into a doorway, albergue Casa Nostra on Calle Real Oriente. The owner, a former pilgrim is sitting at a desk just inside the door. After all the formalities are attended to I present a €10 bill and he goes off to get change, comes back, hands me my change and thanks me 'as gaeilge', that's 'in Irish' to you 'Sassenachs'. He laughs when he sees my reaction and explains that a previous pilgrim had taught him to say thankyou in Irish as he likes to be able to thank people in their own language. What a lovely touch.

The only heating in the dorm is a Super Ser gas heater. It appears to be other guests preferred way of drying their clothes. Mine are soaking. This so called waterproof jacket is not as waterproof as the manufacturer said. I am soaked to the skin and my guide book is sodden. As I sent my surplus gear home with Chris, I only have one set of dry clothes for tomorrow so after a nice hot shower I change into them and try to find a spot around the super ser to hang my belongings without much success.

Up the street is La Taberna, a famous and well known bar among pilgrims but as luck would have it, or should I say bad luck, the cocino (kitchen) has closed and won't be open for meals until 7pm. Its 5 now and I don't relish starving for another two hours but nothing I can do about it. The barman, who speaks pretty good English must have taken pity on me for he offers to make me up a meal from the bar food he has. First he supplies a bowl of hot fish soup. My first thought is 'yeuchh' but it is amazingly very tasty. He then brings me a platter from the food cabinet at the bar which includes some lovely ham along with a side salad and a carafe of tinto. Half way through it as I chew on a piece of delicious jamon, I remember it is Good Friday and should not be eating meat. Hope the Lord didn't mind too much but I decide to finish it rather than waste it. A cup of coffee and I am ready to head back to the albergue but outside it is really chucking it down now and I don't have my jacket with me. Also, it is not easy running in sandals but I make it back to the albergue just minimally wet.

The people who had hung their clothes around the heater are all now back in the dorm. Some of them are the Spanish family from early this morning. Another pilgrim, from Germany I think, is drawing a portrait of one of the girls in the room. The conversation as it normally does in the dorms comes around to the plans for the next day. Itera de la Vega or Boadilla Del Camino for some, straight through to Fromista for others. My only thought is of the very steep 12:1 climb up Alto Mostelares just outside of town. At this point the artist announces that the weather forecast for tomorrow is dry in the morning, torrential rain after lunch. That sounds like another soaking for me and then I will have no dry clothes at all. Again the doubts start to tear at my soul and I no longer want to carry on. I contact home and Chris tells me Margaret is putting a brave face on it but it is tough for her. I think I will pack this in. It is just not worth the pain in my shoulders and back from the rucksack and the pain in my heart from missing my wife. I will carry on for a few more days then as soon as Aer Lingus flights start from Santiago, I will be on a bus for the airport and home. I gave it my best shot and reckon I didn't do too badly. The phrase from one of the Dirty Harry movies comes to mind. '*A man has got to know his limitations*'. I have reached my limit.

I have spoken to Chris and Margaret and the hospitalero, and I am contemplating going back to Burgos tomorrow but for now I will leave it that I am walking to Itera or Boadilla. We will see what the morning brings. When I see what the weather is like and depending on how sore my back is, I will make my decision then.

Buenos Noches y Buen Camino

Castrojeriz back to Burgos

Day Fourteen, Saturday, 30th March (Easter Saturday)

After much soul searching I have decided to give up. I suppose that's what makes my camino different to other pilgrims'. When doubts arose they pushed on, I gave up. So, my camino is over as far as Spain is concerned anyway. My true camino lies back in Ireland with my family. I miss them so much.

The hospitalero told me there was a bus back to Burgos at 8am so once I have everything packed I head down to the bus stop to wait. A man out walking his dog tells me that the bus does not run at the weekend. Not sure how he got that through to me as he had no English but I recognised the word for Monday. What should I do? Should I walk on to Fromista and try to get home from there or should I get a taxi back to Burgos. It won't be cheap but I will spend as much I suppose on albergues and food. Best thing to do is go back up to La Taberna and contemplate it over a cup of coffee. There is a flyer on the notice board for a taxi and in trying to ask the bar owner about it he assumes I want a taxi and phones the number for me. Well, that's the decision made for me then. While I am killing time a Basque couple that I met yesterday come in for breakfast and we get chatting. His English is OK and we get around to politics. Well why not? An Irish Republican and a Basque Separatist, it is impossible to avoid politics. Without going into details, it was very interesting and passed an otherwise lonely hour.

The Basques are a very unusual people. Historians have no idea where they came from and are known only in the north of the Iberian Peninsula and over the Pyrenees into southern France. Their language, Eusketa, is not related to any known language on the face of this planet; it's not Latin based, nor Germanic nor Arabic. In fact they say you have to be born to it, foreigners can't learn it. Neither the French nor Spanish who surround them fully understand them. All I can say from the few I have met is that they are marvellous people, kind and helpful to the peregrino.

During the Falangist rebellion in the mid-1930s, April 26th, 1937 to be precise, Franco's borrowed air force bombed them at Guernica and as it was market day the town was packed and as a result 1645 innocent civilians were murdered. As the world reacted to the full horror of mass murder from the skies, Franco

[69]

claimed no planes were flying that day and that the Basques had dynamited themselves. The Vatican put pressure on him to negotiate and his response was that the only possible solution was the complete annihilation of the Basque race, genocide. It's a funny thing about genocide, generally, those who try it pass on and their victims survive all their efforts. Be it Custer, Hitler, Mussolini, or the Serb leaders whose names are beyond my spelling powers. The people of Guernica were the first to suffer what became known as 'blitzkrieg'. From Guernica to Gaza via Poland, London, Birmingham, Coventry, my own city Belfast, the Ruhr Valley, Dresden, Hiroshima, Nagasaki and Hanoi. Will the world never learn?

Franco however got away with it because he had remained neutral in WWII which was of benefit to the allies in the Mediterranean. After the war, his reward was, with the blessing of the USA, that all his atrocities be swept under the carpet. To the shame of the Catholic Church, the Vatican also turned a blind eye. I still remember well, when I was about seven years old, the Christian Brothers holding him up to us kids as a great Catholic Leader. When he died in 1975 without ever paying for his crimes on this earth, there was mourning in Madrid, the Basques danced in the streets.

These people, who had endured suffering under Franco for 40 years and who would continue to suffer at the hands of successive Spanish governments, kept going, never gave up, never surrendered their fierce pride and here am I, giving up because of a little rain and a lot of home sickness. I hope my Basque friends made it all the way.

At last the taxi arrives but the driver is in no hurry, he wants his coffee too. Apologetically he tells me via my Basque friend that I will have to share the taxi with two other pilgrims. When he picks them up I am delighted to find it's the girl from Persia. She and her friend have reached the end of their holiday and are heading back to Burgos to catch the express train to Madrid then on to their home in Malaga. It means the €50 fare is split three ways which is a lot more affordable for us. I say goodbye to them at the Rosa de Lima railway station and the taxi then drops me at the bus station in town where I can book a ticket to Madrid for Easter Sunday which will be my last day in Spain. There is a bus to the airport at 3:45 with three seats left so I purchase a ticket even though I still do not have a flight home. I need some internet now so a visit to the Tourist Info office is my next port of call. They sign me up for 24 hours free internet that is available in all municipal buildings in Burgos. As the albergue is municipal, it's available there too as I will discover later. I now have a ticket booked with Aer Lingus for 8:30pm tomorrow so nothing else to do but enjoy what is left of my time in Burgos.

As I crossed the plaza heading for the albergue I was almost certain I heard my name being called. I walk on a little further and again I hear my name called. Turning around, I see Elizabeth and Katy 2 running towards me and it is time for hugs again. Big Jim is also in town and is staying in the Marriott Hotel. The Camino the Texan way I laugh. We arrange to meet for dinner that night and then I make my way up to the albergue. I have no sooner settled in than I hear that broad Irish brogue, its Big Phil. He is still crippled with injuries and raw meat where the soles of his feet should be. The skin has all but peeled away but still he goes on. Vying for sainthood he is. The guy doesn't even have a rain jacket anymore, just the hood of it left. If anyone is going to Santiago it is him but I dread to think how he is going to handle that mud on the Meseta.

As I lie on my bunk contemplating the journey I have made, the people I have met and whether I have made the right decision to go home I hear two American girls talking. Now I have met a few Americans on this walk and they have all been the very best of people and nowhere near the stereotypical image Europeans have of Yanks abroad. But this one fits the bill. She is holding court over a couple of admirers and boasting about how far she has walked and how she is carrying 30k of equipment. She is complaining about this albergue because it is too backward to have wi-fi. Another voice, not American, chips in to tell her she must be doing something wrong because the old Irish guy (me) in the next row has his internet connection with no trouble. A wry smile crosses my face as she shouts at them that it is not possible followed by my little comment of '*Oh yes it is*'. Everyone laughs and although I can't see her face, I can imagine how red it must be. I am not about to tell her that the tourist office will sign you up for free wi-fi which is available in all municipal buildings in Burgos and this albergue is municipal. I know I should not be so unkind on the camino but I just can't resist it. Later I see the same girl out on the balcony cooking on her camp stove. She really is carrying way too much.

While using my wi-fi connection I find a message from Sarah that makes me cry. I had to walk 200 miles to find that my

[71]

camino was always back to Ireland and not to Santiago, back with the people I love and who love me. I found a lot of love here in Spain from some fantastic people from all over the world but none as warm as the Basques, Navarones, Catalans and those that are just simply Spanish. I list the Basques etc. separately from Spanish as that's the way they prefer it and as that's what they want then that's what I will do.

So there it is. My camino was from Belfast to London to Biarritz to San Sebastion to Pamplona to Castrojeriz and back to Ireland. Who needs a Compostela when I have what I have at home? My family. Maybe someday I will come back to finish the walk but I have already found that I already have everything a man could want. A wonderful wife and seven marvellous children

Buenos Noches y Buen Camino

A Day in Burgos

Day Fifteen, 31st March, Easter Sunday

I have been kicking around Burgos since before 8am until the bus for Madrid is due. While waiting, I went to mass with Jim Cashion and family and then went for breakfast with Edmund from Norway, whom I met last night at dinner, and Big Phil. Phil has decided to take the bus to Leon as some news from home has restricted his time in Spain so thankfully, he will not have to negotiate the Meseta. As I no longer need it I have given Phil all the food I have left and my poncho to keep him dry. I say goodbye to him for the last time as he goes off to find an albergue for the night and I wander into the plaza and sit down for a beer and try to kill some time. There is a parade in the plaza and a service in front of the cathedral. There is a clergy man there and from his attire I assume he is maybe a cardinal, but he looks forever like our new Pope Francis. The service is over and the plaza empties so no point in sitting here, I may as well go down to the bus station and wait there

It's coming up on 1pm and I am completely bored. I have put my rucksack into its protective carrier bag and just sit here watching the minutes tick by on the clock. I tried to get on an earlier bus but language difficulties led me to believe my ticket was not transferrable. A couple of peregrinos arrive by bus, such cheats I laugh, having done the same myself. Now something odd happens. For some reason, I don't know why, I took out my ticket to look at it. Oh my God! How stupid can one person be? My ticket is for 3:45 to Madrid airport NOT 15:45. I forgot that timetables work on the 24 hour clock. That's what the girl was trying to tell me, I had missed my bus. It must have been Paul or my guardian angel that made me look again. There is still time to book a new ticket for 15:00. There are three seats left luckily but the bus does not stop at the airport. It gets into Madrid at 18:00 hours (note I am now using the 24 hour clock) and then I have to get to the airport.

The bus makes good progress and appears to be ahead of schedule until about 30 miles outside Madrid when everything on the motorway comes to a stop. No accident, no road works, just stopped. I arrive in Madrid in time to see the airport bus pull away from the stop so I will have to get a taxi. That stupid mistake has cost me an extra €40. I arrive in the airport to find an extremely long line at the Aerlingus check in but as I have already checked in, I can go straight to bag drop. I can feel the

[73]

dagger in my back from those in the long line as I drop my bags and head off to security. At least something has gone right today. For once I get through security quickly without setting off any beeps and straight into a café for some dinner and my last café con leche. If all goes according to timetable I will be on the 23:00 bus to Béal Feirste and be home about 1am. Margaret has said she will run me a bath when I get in. Hope she is not joking.

I am on the plane for Ireland now and Spain is a long way behind me. Margaret texted me to check on the time of arrival for the bus from Dublin just after we landed. Not looking forward to another two hours travelling but it is nearly over now. My bag came through pretty quickly so I head for the exit wondering where I get the Belfast bus. The automatic doors open before me and there is Margaret standing waiting for me. I love this marvellous woman. She looks as beautiful now as the day she walked down the aisle. I hug her like I have never hugged her before. Sarah and Sharon have also come down to meet me with Chris driving. Doubt anyone has a better son.

Home at last with just 5 minute left of March. There is a still a lot of snow on the streets so it must have been really rough on Margaret and Sarah. And that bath I mentioned earlier, Margaret has run it for me and then to top it off, when I am finished she has sausages waiting for me. I am a lucky man to have a wife like her

Buen Camino

The End (or is it)

P.S. 22/4/2013

I have just been reading over my notes from the Camino and it brought tears to my eyes. I had thought about going back next spring to complete my walk but Margaret has encouraged me to go back as soon as possible. I have a couple of cruises planned so as soon as they are finished I will return to Spain at the start of September.

I have heard from Jim Cashion since my return. He, Caitlin and Katie along with his wife, Mary, and son, Mason, who joined them at Saria, arrived in Santiago on Friday, April 19th. Congratulations to them. Big Phil and Elizabeth also arrived the day after. Elizabeth carried on to Finnisterre then Muxia, got a bus to Bilbao and started her journey home to Australia. Congratulations to them all

Buen Camino mi amigos

Part Two

St James Gate Dublin

Wednesday, 24th July

Today I took the first step of my second leg to Santiago. Margaret and I visited the Guinness Storehouse, just off St James Road, Dublin. They stamped my pilgrim passport with

the Sello of the St James Confraternity, and another for St James Gate. We then visited the Church of St James just around the corner and got their stamp too. Tomorrow is the feast of St James so I suppose I can say I have started the second leg of my pilgrimage. The 5th September is not far off now but I still have another cruise to Norway to fit in the last week of August. There won't be much time before flying out again so I need to have everything ready before we go.

I suppose I should explain why I went to St. James Gate. This was the traditional starting place for Irish pilgrims going on the camino long before Arthur set up his brewery. As you can see from the photo, the church was established in 1724, some thirty-five years before Guinness arrived. Credit to Guinness though as they continue to stamp the pilgrims credentials to this day. Unfortunately, the tour guides did not know where the name, St James Gate came from but they do now. And they also did not know that the Irish Harp on their cans and bottles is the wrong way round but just threw that in for fun, nothing whatsoever to do with the Camino.

Buen Camino

Off to Bilbao

Thursday, 5th September

This morning I got the early bus for Dublin. It made good time and I was in the airport for 9:40 and through bag drop and security by 10:30. The plane was about 30 minutes late taking off but that was not too bad as I don't have any time restrictions today. I didn't have any restrictions initially on this trip but we have arranged to have a new bathroom fitted and as Margaret does not want to be on her own while the work is carried out, I must be home before the 7th October. That means the latest flight I can get home is 5th October.

I have never seen so many peregrinos outside of an albergue before. This plane is truly a pilgrim flight so it means there are no problems indulging in conversation with the people around me. In Bilbao I got a little worried as my bag was the last one out but no problems in the end. I got a bus into town with a few other pilgrims but I was the only one staying in Bilbao and then starting from Burgos or Castrojeriz depending on bus times tomorrow. Others were starting from other points and some were doing the Camino del Norte. The bus dropped me at the top of the bus station right by the path that leads to the hostel about five minutes' walk away. I have a reservation in the hostel Pil Pil which I must say is a very fine hostel and would recommend to anyone staying overnight in Bilbao. Now for a relaxing walk around town without my rucksack.

Here I go again walking. Dandered round to the Guggenheim and took a few photos especially of the floral dog in front of the museum, Bilbao is a beautiful city. Their football stadium is just behind the hostel so I decide to pay it a visit, the home of Bilbao Atletico. It's not there, just one terrace, the playing field and the floodlights. The rest has been ripped down and the whole thing is being rebuilt. The first match of the season is in ten days' time so they are putting up a great wire fence to make sure the ball stays in the ground. I wish them the best of luck with that.

My first mishap awaits me when I get back to the hostel. Somehow my razor has got switched on in my bag and the battery is almost flat. I know from experience that if I use this razor every second day it will last about three weeks so I had not bothered bringing the charger. Looks like I am growing a beard after all. I am in for the night now which is just as well, it's lashing down outside with thunder and lightning

Buenos Noches y Buen Camino

Bilbao to Burgos

Friday, 6th September

What is it with me and bus timetables? I could have sworn my bus this morning was at 10 so got down to the station early. I could have had another hour in bed as the bus was at 10:45. It is about 13:30 when I eventually arrive in Burgos hoping to get a 14:00 bus to Castrojeriz. Unfortunately that timetable is well out of date and the bus I want isn't until 17:00. That would get me in about 18:00 but would there still be beds in the albergues at that time. I don't think it is worth the risk so I decide to walk the familiar path again. After all, I have done it before and should be fitter and well able for it this time. Well, that's what I tell myself.

The albergue opens at 1pm so I may as well go there, get a bed and drop my bag off. I arrived at the association albergue, Casa del Cubo, at 13:45 to find the first two floors were filled already. When I was here at Easter, they didn't open the 3rd floor at all. At my bunk, I found a small woman, whose language I didn't recognise, was trying to claim it for herself. Now, the numbers are very clearly marked on each bunk so she was just chancing her arm to get a bottom one. If she had asked, she could have had it but the acting dumb routine was not making me conducive to offering.

After I had sorted out my belongings I made my way down to the Black Book for pizza and then round to the river to take some pictures. The trees were in bloom and the river was gently flowing, a bit different to when I was here at Easter.

Back to the albergue for a rest and plan tomorrows walk. There does not seem to be any English speakers on this floor so I don't think there is much chance of making friends tonight. Looks like I will be walking on my own tomorrow. Its 10Km to the first town but it has been a while since I have walked that far so not looking forward to it, but at least there is café facing the albergue that opens at 6am so I will get breakfast before I start. But for now, it's time for dinner.

It is now 20:00 and I am fed and watered and in for the night. Tomorrow the walking begins again and this time, I finish in Santiago de Compostela, no turning back, it is Ultreya this time or to coin an old movie phrase *'Santiago or Bust'*. Hopefully as I know this part of the Camino, it won't seem as hard as last

[79]

time. Looking at the guidebook though is a bit worrying. This albergue holds about 200 souls and is packed but tomorrow's stage has accommodation for around 85 which could be a problem so it might be advisable to stop before Hornillos while everyone else is pushing on. But for now its

Buenos Noches y Buen Camino

Burgos to Rabé de las Calzados

Day 1, Saturday, 7th September

This was supposed to be my starting day from Castrojeriz but so much for plans. I started out early from Burgos and had not reached the city limits when I developed my first blister on the tip of my fourth toe on my right foot. It's not too much of a problem so I will treat it later and just walk on for now. A guy called Sam from the Netherlands slows down to chat for a while and then heads of on his own. The spots of rain earlier have not developed into anything so I reckon I can get my coat off and cool down a little.

I am out of town now and walking on a rough trail. To my right is the big gaol I spotted last time I walked this stretch. Hunger pangs are getting me now so I finish off the crumbs that at one time were Weetabix breakfast biscuits. That café in Burgos was not open, why do they put out signs that say they will be open and then not bother? That's when I heard it. A peel of thunder in the distance, then another. Its heading my way so better get my coat out of the bag before it gets here. As a child I had been taught to count the seconds between the flash and the thunder and that would tell me how many miles away it was. It is getting closer. I have never been afraid of thunder and lightning in my life but when the flash and the bang come together you know you are right underneath the centre of the storm. Found myself praying to Jesus to be on one side of me and Paul on the other. That's when the rain hit. Well, my new jacket works well and keeps me dry, up top anyway. Unfortunately I am wearing shorts and the water is running down my legs and into my boots. There is an underpass below the highway at Villabilla and I can go no further as it is packed tight with other pilgrims. While I wait for the logjam to clear, I have a drink and an energy tablet then set off again and with my poles extended, I am setting a good pace and actually passing other people, a first for me. Where is my water bottle? Damn it, I have left it in the underpass about 1km back. I can't go on without it, water is too important so nothing for it but to go back. Now I am back in my usual position, tail end Charlie.

By the time I make Tarjados my socks and boots are soaking so after something to eat in the local café I need to change my socks, nothing I can do about the boots. On to Rabé and the new socks are wet too. I stop at the first bar as I enter town to get directions to the albergue and the bar owner offers me a

Miraculous Medal and is surprised to see I am already wearing one. He didn't realise that it is known the world over and not just in Spain. Seems there is a monastery in town that blesses them and they are handed out to passing peregrinos by the bar owner and the hospitaleros.

The albergue is not yet open so I get my boots off and lay the insoles down in the sun to dry. When I eventually get in and get a bed I discover that the rain has got into my rucksack and most of my underwear is wet. The hospitalero has a bundle of newspapers so that pilgrims can stuff them in their boots to dry them and there is an airer at the side of the building so everything is hung up and there is good drying in the afternoon sun.

This albergue provides dinner and breakfast so I can relax and not worry about finding somewhere to eat. Time to treat that blister; I pierce it and leave a thread in to wick away any more fluid. To ensure its clean I pour on a little whiskey (medicinal purposes only) and it stings like hell. Terrible waste of good whiskey. And now for more bad luck, my sleeping bag and liner are also wet. Not much I can do about the bag but the liner can be hung up in the sun. Hopefully it will be dry by bedtime.

An Irish family arrived and we all had dinner together and headed down to the monastery/convent (in Spain the one word, monastery, covers both) as someone had told us there was a vigil Mass for tomorrow. Unfortunately even in Spain there is a shortage of priests so no Mass tonight. The nuns however invite us into the little chapel to pray for the Popes special intentions for that weekend, peace in Syria. They then gave us the pilgrims blessing and more medals. So glad I stopped here for the night. There is a church bell pealing every hour. Is it to continue all night? A new pilgrim arrives in the dorm and it turns out he is also Irish. He has walked from St Jean in just over a week. He is soaking wet as he got caught in another thunder storm. There were hailstones and he has brought one in, it is the size of a golf ball. I wouldn't fancy getting hit by one of those. There are so many Irish in here and other albergues that I wonder who is left at home to look after the Auld Island.

The bell has stopped; it did not ring at 10pm. There is an agreement with the albergues that there will be no ringing between 10pm and 7am

Buenos Noches y Buen Camino

[82]

Rabé de las Calzados to Hontanas

Day 2, Sunday, 8th September

After a reasonable breakfast I headed out into the darkness of a late summer morning just as the 7am church bells began to ring. I had to walk slowly and use the light from my head torch to follow the signs until the sky started to brighten about 7:30. By 8:00 I had climbed to the top of the Meseta, 950m, and making good time towards Hornillos del Camino. The weather was dull and cool, cool enough to not take my coat off. Shortly before entering the town at 9am, the Irish family passed me by. They seemed to be on a schedule and had the Parador hotel in Leon as their goal but I caught up with them again at a shop in town where we all stopped to buy some food for later. A couple of Spanish ladies who had just come out of a hostel stop to chat and it is they who tell me that the Spanish do not carry a shell to Santiago, they only bring them back.

As the Irish family pushed on, I stopped at a bar popular with peregrinos, Casa Manolo, for my usual morning café con leche. A Catalan from Barcelona was already there. I had met him last night in the albergue and again this morning when he stopped and offered to take a picture of me with the Meseta in the background. For some strange reason, he was carrying his rucksack on the front. As he was leaving he bought a packet of two chocolate rolls and gave me one then off he went. He had started from Barcelona three weeks ago but I would never see him again but I hope he made it all the way. Outside the bar there is a square with patio tables so I stop at one to tend to a little blister. Just as I finish rubbing some of the Vaseline type pilgrim's balm into my feet, a French couple stop as the lady has a bad blister problem so I gave them some antiseptic wipes and a blister plaster.

Now it was time to ascend the second part of the Meseta, climbing it twice in the one morning is not a great idea. Another pilgrim I met yesterday, Joy from Pittsburgh caught up on me, said hello and stormed on. Not many this time seem to have the time to slow down and talk for a few minutes. I am really feeling tired now but from previous experience, I know that we will drop down into a river valley and then have another steep climb up to 950m again. Think I will stop at that river valley at the San Bol albergue.

[83]

Every step is now an ordeal. Don't know why John Brierly goes on so much about the Meseta, it has not been kind to me this time or back at Easter. If I never see it again it will be too soon. At last the turn off for San Bol but there is a sign that says it won't open until 14:00 and its only midday now. What to do? There is a patch of mown grass that provides a nice spot to lie down to rest and think. After a short rest and a big peach inside me, I feel somewhat refreshed and decide to push on to Hontanas, another 5km further on. I have already covered 13.5km this morning so I should be able to do another 5. As I am about to set off, a Danish girl stops to check that I am OK. We talk for a few minutes then she and her friend head on but 3km later I come upon them having a picnic and they invite me to join them. I have to decline as the backpack is killing me and if I stop I will never get started again but she gives me a chocolate oatcake to eat as I walk, wishes me well and off I go. I never saw her again.

Hontanas is situated just below the summit so it can't be seen from a distance, the church tower just suddenly appears and it is a very welcome sight. Into the albergue Santa Brigida and first job after a shower is to empty my bag and try to figure out why it is dropping to the left and pulling the back out of me. The left support bar has come out of its Velcro so if it happens again I will take both out of position. I want to treat my feet with some of Christopher's foot balm but it's gone. I must have left it behind when I applied some back in Hornillos. I will have to buy a new tub next time I see it.

Well, I am all showered and changed, blisters treated and the sleeping bag hung up to finish drying. I won't need it tonight as blankets are supplied here and it's so warm now, the liner should be all I need. Funny thing about that liner, it's the only thing I have been unable to get back into its stuff bag so I just stow it in an Argos bag.

As this albergue is another that supplies dinner there is no need to go looking for a café so I take the time to go for a stroll. The Danish and Canadian ladies I met last night are staying here too. The Canadian has a spare dry sac that is only taking up space so she offers it to me to prevent any more clothes getting wet in the rucksack. It was a big help throughout the rest of the Camino so I am very grateful to her.

Dinner was great. Ensalada followed by paella. The company was just as good. Danish, Canadian, South Korean, German,

American, Dominican Republic and me. The guy from the Dominican Republic by the way was the one walking with the Danish girl earlier in the day. I had thought they were friends but they had just been walking together for the day and she had decided to push on to Castrojeriz

Buenos Noches and Buen Camino

Hontanas to Castrojeriz

Day 3, Monday, 9th September

During the night I awoke with severe cramp pains in both legs. Like nothing I have ever felt before and so bad I thought I would not be able to carry on. I really did too much over the Meseta yesterday. However, morning brings new light and new hope, the pain has gone. The power of prayer once again amazes me. I have never been particularly religious. I do the minimum required of me and no more but I find myself praying an awful lot more now. When I say praying I mean talking to God as if he was just another peregrino, not formal prayers that someone else has written.

There is no need to start off in the dark today as it is an easy walk into Castrojeriz so I can treat myself to an extra hour in bed. Last time, todays walk felt like forever in the rain but this time in the warm early morning sun it's no more than a stroll and I can take the trail rather than the road. It is easier on the feet walking on trails as opposed to tarmac.

I thought I might carry on over the next climb after a coffee in La Taberna, the popular bar in the centre of town but to my dismay, it is closed, so water and biscuits will have to suffice. I have treated the blister on my heel while waiting hopefully for the bar to open, but eventually it becomes clear it is not going to happen so it's time to move on. Ouch! When I try walking on the blister it's like a needle sticking into me. The problem is the foot bed in the boot. There is a little bit of damage to it just where I am getting the blister. I wonder if there is anywhere I can buy new ones. The albergue I had stayed in last time is closed until 14:00 so I may as well check out the one at the top of the town. It is open and fairly empty so I decide to stay here for the night, best to rest this blister than try to climb another Meseta on it. As luck would have it there is a sports store next door so I purchase new insoles; hope they do the trick. Tried La Taberna one more time but it is still closed and I never found out why.

Lunch in a local café right beside the albergue is not bad. A bocadillo with omelette and a glass of wine for €3.60. A group of Canadians arrive but they seem more like the stereotypical 'yanks abroad' though of all the Americans I have met, only one girl fitted that stereotype. I am glad I got in early; most people are sleeping on mattresses on the floor. Also in the room are some Irish, Sean, JP and Gregg. Sean and JP are travelling with a Geordie of Irish descent called Frank. He is waiting on word of the birth of his grandchild who is due today so I lent him my phone to call home to see if the baby had been born yet but he can't get through. Gregg had seen my name in the guest book and came looking for me. Seems there was an Irish athlete of the same name and Gregg had been his coach and he thought he was renewing an old friendship so I think I was a bit of a disappointment to him.

At dinner time Frank invites me to join them so off we go in search of a good restaurant. While checking out two establishments we met a Canadian lady of Irish descent, Siobhan, who was on her own so we invited her to join us. The craic as they say was 90, the wine was flowing and Frank was singing. When we paid our bill and headed back to the albergue it was decided that another bottle of wine was needed so we stopped at the local bar. Once again the singing commenced and the locals seemed unsure as to what to make of these mad Irishmen. The time slipped away until it was past time for lights out. Just then I looked up to see a somewhat upset hospitalero out looking for his lost sheep and he somewhat angrily herded us back to the dormitory. What a night!

Buenos Noches and Buen Camino

Castrojeriz to Itero de la Vega

Day 4, Tuesday, 10th September

Today is, once again, an early start. I am on the road before 7am so the head torch is a must. It's a good job it's dark as I approach Alto Mostelares. Out of sight, out of mind, as they say. It's only 900m, that's 40 to 50m less than the Meseta but it's really steep, 1:12. As usual on an incline, everyone is passing me by. Looking back at the spectacular sunrise breaking over the hill at Castrojeriz is really beautiful, but for once it's a beauty I can do without. If God had just given me an uphill gear I could really enjoy this beauty of creation. In the guide book the path appears to be fairly straight but there are quite a few twists and turns and at each one I think to myself, 'is the summit just around this one'. Well, after many stops to catch a breath, have a drink and ask Jesus to get behind me and push, the summit is at last just ahead. There is a covered rest area where I can drop my bag and take some pictures and then have a snack but, boy, is it cold. At this altitude, the sweat cools down very quick and shedding layers just now is not a great idea. At this point I am joined by a Filipino lady and her two American born daughters. One of them, Jessica, starts to take off layers and when I advise against it, her mother chips in with an 'I told you so'. Seems she is a nurse and had been trying to tell them about cooling down too fast all morning. As we set off, Jessica stays with me for quite a way to have a chat while her mother and sister take off at speed, well, speed compared to how fast I walk. This trip has been a birthday present for the mother who will be turning 70 in a couple of days. The way she moves makes me look like 90. Anyway, Jessica decides eventually that she had better leave and catch up with her Mom who is disappearing into the distance and once again I am on my own. Sean from last night's shenanigans now catches up and after a few words says he is moving on too.

At last I arrive in the next picnic site, Fuente del Piojo. A man has set up a little kitchen beside the fountain and is serving coffee and bananas and oranges. Initially I thought he had a nice little business idea here but no, he is doing this out of the goodness of his heart. If you want, you can leave a donation but it's purely voluntary. Can't see any peregrino not making a donation but either way, it's a lovely touch. I will see more of these charitable touches in the days to come. The Filipinos and Sean are also at the site but are preparing to leave as I arrive so once again, it's just a few friendly words and they are on their way.

It's only 3.5km to Itero de la Vega and I have decided that that will be enough for today. It's really getting warm today and I am very tired after this morning's steep climb. After a short 1.5km walk, I come across Ermito de San Nicolas. It's an albergue all on its own in the middle of nowhere. It is run by an Italian Confraternity but it has no electricity, in fact it has nothing but a shower and toilet out the back. It's also donativo. There is a bench outside so I sit down and ponder the idea of staying here. Eventually I decide it is too early to stop and I head on. I regret that decision sometimes as I later seen a video on the internet about this place and it looked like it was well worth staying in. If I ever go back, I think I will stop here.

At last, I trudge into Itero and as I pass a café, Puente Fitero, which is also an albergue, I hear someone call my name. It's the Filipinos so I join them for a coffee and a chat. Their plan is to make it to Fromista but that's too far for me so we say our farewells and off they go. I never met them again but it seems they were well known along the route and I met others who told me of their progress. This albergue is not yet open so maybe the next one is, so off I go. La Mochila is open so that's my bed for the night. It's a restaurant as well as an albergue so I am fixed for dinner and breakfast once again. For now I have the dorm all to myself. Some Germans have come in but opted for private rooms but I am happy with a bunk for €6.

It's been a fairly lonely day for walking and the Germans are keeping to their own company, very little interaction. One lady that I do get talking to tells me she has been living in Bordeaux for 30 years even though she is German. She also tells me about an event in Pamplona last week. Over 600 pilgrims arrived in town and there wasn't a spare bed anywhere. I will need to pick up my pace if I am to stay ahead of that lot for long.

Dinner was good as usual with a nice bottle of wine. The company is made up of Australians, Americans and Indonesians. When I get back to the room I find I have been joined by a group of Catalan cyclists and they apologise for the noise but, hey, they have just arrived and need to get themselves sorted. They tell me about a big event in Catalonia where everyone will join hands in a show of solidarity for Catalan independence and they hope to make it the longest line of people holding hands that the world has ever seen. As we will all be on the road tomorrow, we all hold hands in the dorm before turning in for the night

Buenos Noches y Buen Camino

Itero to Fromista

Day 5, Wednesday, 11th September

It is now a week since I returned to Spain. I have not got as far as I had hoped or planned for. I have only started and already I am two to three days behind schedule. Oh well, the best laid plans of mice and men as they say. I will just have to take each day as it comes.

I started out at 7am and its pitch black but that's ok at first as there are some town lights but as I get further out it becomes as black as a coal mine, not that I have ever been down a coal mine to see how black it is. The Australian couple that I shared dinner with last night are just ahead of me but they stop at a fountain to fill their bottles and I go on ahead. Just outside the town, a tarmac road cuts across my path and I can't see any yellow arrows to point the way. My built in sense of direction tells me it is not to the left but do I turn right or go straight on. I really should have scouted the way out of town last night. There is nothing for it but to get the backpack off and dig out my guide book even though I am fairly certain it is straight on. Satisfied that the direction is indeed straight ahead I sling the pack back up on my back and disaster strikes. I have forgotten to zip up the top pocket and everything falls to the ground including my hip flask. To my horror, the top has broken off and my good Irish whiskey is seeping into the Spanish soil. I should have known better than to put the good stuff into a hip flask designed and marketed for a well-known brand of inferior American stuff. Oh well, no point crying over spilt whiskey, well actually there is every point, but this is not the time to feel sorry for myself. Sure it was only for medicinal purposes anyway. Who am I trying to kid? But a little bit of Spanish soil just outside Itero de la Vega will be forever Irish.

I set off along the track and the sky is starting to lighten up a bit. The Australian couple have just passed me and head off into the distance. They are not walking that fast as to get out of eyesight and I can see them stopping now and then and looking back at the sunrise. Now according to the book this is a pretty flat stage with just one minor and not very steep hill. I can see the Australians top the crest of that hill and look back once again. About ten minutes later I reach the crest myself and can see a long straight path ahead stretching for miles but there is no sign of the Aussies. How could they have gotten out of sight so quickly? They must have taken to running. I never saw them again. However the further I go with no sign of any other human beings, the more I start to think I have missed a turn and that's where the Aussies went. I am looking for signs, every tree and every rock, but there are no yellow arrows. Then I spot a reassuring sign, little holes, lots of little holes, the tell-tale sign of walking poles and eventually a broken pole by the side of the path so I must be on the right track. Now I can concentrate on walking and stop worrying. Just as well as I need to pay attention to the conditions underfoot. This path is 90% flat but still tough going. It is a farm track but the 'pebbles' are the size of spuds. A couple of times I have gone over on my left ankle and only I have been using walking poles I could easily have sprained it.

Exactly two hours after starting out I walk into the albergue in Boadilla del Camino. It is also a restaurant so I want to get my second breakfast. The one in Itero was not very filling. Sitting at the table is a Dutch girl called Nicole. She has hurt her foot so is staying for a second night. I will meet her again. After about an hour I hit the road again for my destination for today, Fromista.

It's a pleasant walk along the Canal de Castilla. I stop for a little snack and to take in the beauty of the place but as I start off again I can feel that damned blister again. As long as I keep going I don't feel it but give it a rest and it complains bitterly when I start again. Gradually, I start slowing up again as a recurring pain in my right calf and back of my knee starts acting up again. Not to worry though, Fromista is literally just around the corner. I have opted to stay at the first albergue, a converted railway station right beside the tracks. Its €15 but that includes dinner so it's a good deal. Trouble is, there is no one else here. Suppose it's not everyone's cup of tea due to its proximity to the railway track but I quite like the sound of trains. In the bar/restaurant part there is also a craft shop.

Very tempted to buy Margaret a hand carved wooden bendy animal but I doubt it would survive the journey.

I went for a walk into town and found a nice little bar on the shady side of the street so treated myself to a cold beer. On the way back, I spotted a supermarket so decided it was time to top up my food supplies. I got two bananas, a packet of BabyBel cheese, chorizo and orange juice for the princely sum of €5. I will need the supplies as tomorrow it's a 20km hike, the longest I have done this trip. Hope I can make it. I covered 15km today in 4.5 hours including a one hour stop for breakfast. I reckon then that if I do the first 10km in approximately 2 hours and the second 10 in three to four hours then by starting out at 7am I should reach my destination around 14:00. Think I will take the sendo route. May be boring but it will be the easier walk and the shortest distance but we shall see what tomorrow brings.

I had a very good dinner but on my own for the first time. There was a husband and wife booked in but they opted for a private room at the back. One Spaniard has joined me in the dorm but I speak a lot more Spanish than he does English and you could write down what I know on the back of a postage stamp. I will meet him a few times along the way and our only communication will be friendly waves. Later on as I am settling down for the night an American lad arrives in. He has just done 50km today. He wanted to test his body as he says. What would he have done if his body had failed the test I say? Oh well its lights out for another day

Buenos noches y Buen Camino

Fromista to Carrión de los Condes

Day 6, Thursday, 12th September

I set out at 6:30 this morning. The hospitalero spotted me leaving and ran after me and although he had no English he conveyed the message that they owned a bar in town and if I could wait a few minutes he would get it open and ready for breakfast. After a small but pleasant meal I got on the road at just after 7:00. I am feeling good this morning and I am covering a lot of ground fairly fast, although, as I know my own capabilities, I am aware it won't last.

At Población de Campos there is a choice of route. Turn to the right and follow a river path to Villalcázar de Sirga or keep left and walk the sendo along the road. It may sound trivial, but the river route is about 2km longer and as I have not done a Brierly day this time, I feel that any added extras might be pushing it a bit so I opt to take the road to Revenga de Campos.

It's a pleasant enough walk and I meet a couple of Australian sisters that I first met back in Itero. In Revenga there is a nice little rest area in the centre of town with picnic tables and a fountain and an unusual metal sculpture of a traditional peregrino. Time for a snack methinks so I waste a little time relaxing in the early morning sun. Nothing is opened yet so the usual café con leche is not available. As I head on down the road towards the next town I spy a mother waiting at a bus stop with her two children all dressed for school and it reminds me of how I always hated this time of year going back to school after the summer holidays. For some reason even though I am now 64, I still have a dislike of September and feel sorry for those kids. As I pass on the other side of the road they shout out *'Buen Camino'* and wave just as they are about to get on the school bus that has just arrived. I really appreciated that. The sun is really coming up now and although the fields to the side look great bathed in long rays of the rising sun, the road to my left is really boring. Maybe I should have taken the river route.

At last I arrive in Villalcázar and the heat is really getting to me today. There has been no shade along the sendo to break it up a little. There is a nice green area at the front of the town where I can sit down and have a bite to eat. I have hiked a good 15km this morning; I have walked this far before but didn't have another 5 to go. I am not feeling as good as I did this morning when I started out. I have taken to counting the distance markers along the roadside and trying to count the time between each one. I estimate that I am doing no more than 3km per hour so it's going to be almost two hours to walk just over 5km. I feel absolutely shattered at this point so I rest a little longer this time and drink a little more than usual while I pass the time of day with a trio of French ladies before moving on.

At last I can see Carrión at the bottom of the hill but it's a very long hill down into town. There is a man walking up the hill towards me and he is stopping each pilgrim that he meets. Is this another scrounger like we met at Logroño? Well, he isn't scrounging; he is using a broken walking pole to scratch out directions to his albergue. If it isn't the first one I come to he has no chance of my custom. I am really struggling now and other peregrinos are stopping to give me encouragement and urge me on as they pass by. Is it that obvious that I am almost in a state of collapse? A group of Irish pass by and tell me to join them for a pint that night but they didn't stay in the same albergue and I never met them again.

The first albergue is a convent, Santa Clara. I assume the nuns are what we call in Ireland, the Poor Clares. The hospitalero communicates with them via an intercom and we never seen a single one of them which leads me to believe that given the name Santa Clara and what appears to be an enclosed order, they must indeed be the Poor Clares. The hospitalero shows me into my bed for the night and where to find the key for the door. In the kitchen there are boxes of fruit, vegetables and pastries and he tells me these are with the compliments of the nuns. What a lovely gesture.

Later in the day I met my Canadian and Danish friends that I first met back in Rabé. They told me about a market in the town where they had bought some food but when I went looking it was long over. Found a supermercado though and replenished my supplies. It was a nice walk though through a nice town. However my scouting of the route realises my fears. It is a steep climb out of town in the early morning. On my way back, I see a shop selling the foot balm I want but it is closed. Hopefully it will be open later.

Seems there is a pilgrim mass in the church tonight so instead of looking for a restaurant I throw together a makeshift meal. A tomato from the nuns' supply, a tin of tuna, half a bag of fruit and nut and a BabyBel cheese. Does not sound very appetising but I enjoyed it. I washed it down with a cup of tea and one of the complimentary pastries.

I got down to the church just as benediction was ending and mass starting. There are a lot of people here that all seem to know someone else in the congregation but I see no-one I know. There is a young Asian priest assisting and I am informed he is from Korea and is walking the Camino. He plans to stay here for a few days and minister to pilgrims passing through. At the end of mass the local priest asks for all pilgrims to remain in the church. There is a man in what I would guess to be, his fifties who is translating for him. He prays for and with us and then each pilgrim steps forward, says their name and where they are from and the priest gives them an individual blessing. We are all given a little paper star to remind us of the heavens and where we are going. I have kept it safe and still have it. I will treasure it always. At the front of the group I can see a lady with a broad brimmed hat very American in style but my assumption that she is American is way off the mark. She is from Leitrim in Ireland.

I checked that shop for the foot balm after Mass but unfortunately it never reopened.

It's been a tough day. This is the furthest I have walked this trip although I did a similar distance at Easter but not in the blazing sun of today. Approximately 4.5 hours walking with two 15 to 20 minute breaks, that's about 4.5km/hr, not as slow as I had thought earlier. My first Brierley day of this trip but tomorrow will not be another one. 18km will do me as opposed to Brierley's guide recommending 27. I am feeling a whole lot better as I slip into bed

Buenos Noches y Buen Camino

[96]

Carrión to Calzadilla de la Cueza

Day 7, Friday, 13th September

Today I started at 6:40. Somebody's alarm went off just after 5:00 so I thought I might as well get up. I made some of the porridge that I had brought from home but it was so disgusting, I nearly threw up. What is it about Spanish water? I have eaten these pre-packed oats many times before but the couple of times I have made it in Spain, it has tasted really foul. Oh well, there are still some of those jam buns supplied by the nuns so I pinch a couple and make my way into town to find a bar and get some coffee. There is a sign in the bar that there is a bus to Leon at 11:45. Boy, am I sorely tempted? While I am enjoying my coffee, the guy who interpreted at mass last night came in so I started a conversation with him and confided that I am really worried about finding a bed at night as the number of peregrinos seems to be increasing by the day. This is where I got the best advice of my time on the Camino. He told me that he always started around 6 to 6:30 walked for six hours and then stopped at the first albergue he came to. He has walked the camino three times, all at the busiest time of year, and has never had a problem getting a bed. Later that day I will see some graffiti that will echo his words.

It is time to get on the road again, so I pay my bill and get the backpack on. There is a nice way of doing things here in Spain. You place your order for coffee and sit down and enjoy it, same with beer. It is only when you have finished that you pay *la cuenta*, the bill. Can you see that ever taking off in any bar in Belfast, or any bar anywhere?

It is still dark as I start but in the town centre there is enough light from the street lighting. However, it's not long before I am walking in the pitch black again. Just outside town, I come across a group standing at a roundabout wondering which way to go. Some say straight ahead and some Aussies say to the right. Well, I have just seen a sign that clearly said straight ahead. A Dubliner seems to be the leader here but he is not leading too well. He like the others missed the sign and won't take my word for it so he runs across the road looks around and shrugs his shoulders. I have no time for this so I cross the road and there for all to see is a big yellow arrow. How on earth did he miss it? Stupid Dub! Only joking Dubliners.

In his guide book, John Brierley says the sendos are boring and trails are best. This trail is without a doubt the most boring part I have come across so far, more so than any sendo. Mile after mile of flat fields with nothing to see and dust, lots of dust, especially when a farm vehicle drives by. The map shows three picnic sites along the way and I have chosen to stop at the first and third for food and drink. Just before the first stop there is a little dog skipping about so I cut off a piece of my chorizo for it and have acquired a friend for life. It follows me all the way to the first rest area and sits down waiting for more food. Another pilgrim offers it some also and did I say a friend for life, it prefers the other person's food and off it goes with her. Traitor!

The guide book says there are no facilities along the trail but it's not quite right. At a couple of places, some enterprising folk have set up portable road side cafés which are doing a roaring trade but I have brought my own supplies so no point in spending more money with them. As I walk along I realise that there is no one near me. There is a sizeable group ahead and another way behind and every now and then someone from the group behind passes me by and merges with the group ahead. I always seem to be in the middle. Eventually I reach the last rest area where I find the graffiti that has given a name to my journal, 'Walk with the Sun Till ur Shadow Disappears'. It echoes the advice given to me this morning by the Spanish interpreter at last night's mass and it will become my 'modus operandi' for the rest of my Camino. It is good advice and it really works.

Everyone thinks that the sun is at its highest and hottest at midday but here in Spain it seems to be nearer to two in the afternoon, hence the time for siesta I assume, so stopping about 13:00 seems to be a good idea. I will find out tomorrow just how good an idea it is.

I have seen some strange forms of transport along the way. Yesterday a guy skied past on roller blades, today I am overtaken by a man pushing his three year old twins in a double buggy. He is a Scot who lives in Norway but he tells me that his kids are American. I must have looked puzzled because he explains that the children were born by a surrogate he found in the USA so there is no mother. In the past I would have been horrified by this but these two kids are so happy and well behaved and obviously so loved, how can it be wrong? This camino can change your perspective of many things. The couple walking with him are Asian or so I assume so I ask them what country they are from. Yes perspectives can change, not every person with Asian features is from China or South East Asia. Makes me feel almost racist assuming he was from a foreign land further away than the one on Irelands own doorstep, the off shore island we call Britain. They are all stopping at Calzadilla too but the Scot has arranged for a hire car to be there for him. He will drive to Sahagún, stay in a hotel and then drive back in the morning to continue walking. Albergues are not equipped for toddlers.

The albergue here is fantastic. It is run by a Hungarian lady who came on the Camino some years ago and never went home. She is a masseuse so some people are availing of the service. I am covered in dust and tired but in pretty good shape so no need for me to try it. However, I wish I had brought swimming trunks as it's a really hot afternoon and there is a great swimming pool in the back garden, a really first class albergue. Just around the corner there is a hostel/bar/restaurant owned by the same people who own the albergue so I won't have far to go for dinner and a little visit now for a cold beer and a snack, after showering of course, seems very indulgent.

On a hill above the town there is an old monastery. It was deconsecrated many years ago but the very ornate altar was moved to the church in the town. It is a must visit for a photo opportunity and you can get an extra sello here.

Back in the albergue there is an American girl who is trying to explain her name to another pilgrim. He keeps calling her Charlie but her name is Jolly. She eventually says '*Jolly,*' as in '*have a holly jolly Christmas.*' That made me laugh. Later on as I am walking back from the bar, in the middle of a glorious Spanish summer's day, I found myself singing, 'Have a Holly Jolly Christmas'. When I told her about it she had a good laugh.

[99]

For some reason she asks if it's OK to call me Terr. Yea, that's OK with me and I will hear it again a few more times in the days to come. I also met an Irish girl today, Susan from Middleton in Cork along with her Dutch friends Franz and Johann. I will meet them again also.

Dinner was excellent as usual and the company was great. French, Scots and Irish with a few others that I didn't quite get, enjoying a meal together. The Scotsman believe it or not has the same name as me only in reverse, he is Patrick Terence.

Well, off to bed. The bar has told us they will be serving breakfast at 6am so another early start, I am really getting used to rising early. Sahagún is the goal for tomorrow. I might get the bus from there to Leon to catch up on lost time as I am really falling behind my schedule. I had planned to be in or close to Leon by now so at this rate I will never make it to Santiago before the 5th October to catch the flight back to Dublin. I have put a deadline on myself that I must be home for the 7th when the new bathroom is being installed. My original plan to walk on to Finisterre has long since been abandoned. Oh well, tomorrow is another day with enough of its own problems without worrying about something more than two weeks in the future

Buenos Noches y Buen Camino

Calzadilla to Sahagún

Day 8, Saturday, 14th September

It is one week since I started walking and I have covered 105.7km (66ml) an average of 15.1km per day. I really need to step this up a bit to an average of 20km per day if I am ever to reach Santiago.

After a good breakfast at 6am I was on the road for 6:40 with the intention of stopping for coffee in Ledigos, about 6.5km away. Just outside the town there is a map carved in a huge stone showing 4 options. As it is still dark I am having trouble reading it even with my headlamp which seems to be running out of battery. Two other pilgrims had passed me a little way back so I try to listen to see if I can hear them and go the same way but there is not a sound to be heard. The map seems to indicate the best way is to keep right so that's the way I go. Later when the sun comes up and I consult my guide book, I find that although I have gone the right way, turning left would have been the better trail. It's a lonely path and no-one passes and as I walk the sendo, there is not even the sound of a car to break the monotony. All the other pilgrims must have taken the woodland way. As I approach Ledigos I find an amazing arrow.

 It's about 2m long and 1m wide and it has been very carefully put together with stones. I can't believe any pilgrim would have taken the time to do this so it must have been done by local people. The locals really do care about the peregrinos passing by their villages; it's not all about the money they spend.

After my morning café con leche, I fill my water bottles at the local playground and set of for Terradillos de Templarios. This town is traditionally known as the halfway point for those who started in St Jean and as the name suggests, this was a stronghold for the Knights Templar. Nothing remains of their legacy other than the name of the village, the river, Arroyo de Templarios and a huge red cross painted on the side of the albergue. Across the street there is a picnic site and fountain. I have walked in with a guy from Tipperary who insists on singing the old British army marching song, *'It's a Long Way to Tipperary'*. Later I will find out that he has done this with everyone he has met. He has told me that news from home tells him that all the flights out of Santiago are almost full and the prices have gone up. Not what I want to hear and it fills me with a fear that I may not be able to get home when I want to. Sometime later I will find out that he is full of it and there is no problem getting a flight, but for now I am worried. Nothing I can do about it however but continue putting one foot in front of the other and trust in God. I find that I am thinking more and more like this as the miles roll by. I am having conversations with Jesus just as if he was another pilgrim on the way. The Camino really does change people. Is it turning me into a spiritual being? Naw, not really, but I am thinking more and more about my faith in God.

As I leave Terradillos after a little snack, I spot a donkey and a young man dressed in what appears to be riding gear so stop to take a photo. I assume that they are together but as I will find out later, they are not. I will meet that donkey more than once along the way but not the young man. Turns out he is from Brazil and is riding a horse all the way and at times I will find myself following a trail of his horses manure but without ever seeing them. It at least told me I was on the right road.

Today is not a good day. Just as my fitness levels are rising, so does the mercury. Temperatures are soaring to 40C and it's like walking in an oven. I am taking more breaks for rest, water, food and sock changes. At one stop in Moratinos, Susan and Franz go by and ask if I am OK. I am not really but what can they do so I say I am fine. Since the Meseta the terrain has been quite boring and mostly flat with little or no shade. I wonder how the Irish Brigadistas managed to live fight and die in these conditions. They surely were men made of sterner stuff than I.

Just before entering San Nicolás del Real Camino there is a building site with a sign that must be a one off in this entire world. It is of a person hunkering down to do a poo with a red line through it. This is definitely not a place for pilgrims to relieve themselves. Like everyone else passing by, I stop to take a picture. Just around the corner in the centre of the village there is a little bar doing a roaring trade. Susan, Franz, Maurinus and the Scot with his twins have all stopped here for refreshments so I join them. Not because I am looking for some craic, I am shattered walking in this heat and the backpack is really bothering me. April definitely appears to be the better time to be walking even if it does rain and get muddy.

[102]

I am the last to set off after tending to my feet again. They are not blistered but in this heat they feel like they are on fire. The path to Sahagún is hot and dusty and I come across the Scots family again as they have stopped for a little break but I push on after saying hello. In the distance I can see Sahagún but it never seems to get any closer and just when it does appear closer the trail turns off to the right and seems to be going away from town rather than towards it. It is hot, I am really struggling now and praying that the building I see in front of me is an albergue. It's not, but there is a guy on a scooter giving out leaflets for one and he tells me it's about another two kilometres. I think this is the Spanish equivalent of our Irish country mile. It goes on forever. I have met a young American who tells me he is on his last day and must return home tomorrow. It has been his 21st birthday this week and he tells me that some friends are waiting for him along the road. One of them turns out to be Jolly from last night. Don't know when they passed me as they were still in the albergue when I left.

At last, I am in Sahagún and walking through a commercial district close to the railroad tracks. I come to a junction with a sign pointing along the Camino for the municipal albergue, 500m it says but to the right, off the camino, there is a sign for a private one, 300m. I am so tired that that extra 200m seems like miles so I plump for the private one. It is now 14:30, the sun is at its hottest and I have been on the road for eight hours, much longer than I had planned.

The albergue Viatoris appears to be part hotel. There is a proper hotel style reception desk just outside a very nice looking restaurant. Before checking in, the young girl at the desk gives me a bottle of water and tells me to sit down and enjoy it first. It has been so hot today that all pilgrims are being greeted this way. Eventually I get checked in and shown to the albergue part of the building where rather than go for a shower right away, I crash on the bed for half an hour to try and recover. This has been a tough day and convinces me that walking the Camino in July and August is not a very good idea.

Ablutions finished and pack sorted out for tomorrow it's time to explore. There is a famous Elvis themed bar in town that I want to visit but as I step out from under the patio area at the front of the hotel, a suffocating hot air hits me. It's now 16:00 and it seems hotter than it was at noon. The Elvis bar is stroked off my itinerary and I go back in. There in the foyer are all the people I have met this last day or two. Susan, Franz, Johan,

[103]

Maurinus, the Scots family and an Austrian girl whose name I have lost. After spending some time with them they head off for a nap and I venture out to find the railway station. Its 2 to 3 days hike to Leon and one day of it is a horrible hike through the city itself. A few folk who have walked the Camino before are saying that this is the last place to get a train if we are to avoid the city walking. There are two trains tomorrow, one at 8am and the next at 12:45 and both would allow me enough time to get some walking done rather than stay in Leon. I think the early one will do as I may be able to get to mass before moving on. On the way back from the station I meet the Scottish guy and he invites me to have dinner with them tonight at 19:30. Sounds good to me, dinner in the restaurant with good company, can't ask for better than that. Just realised that yesterday was Friday 13th and nothing bad happened even though I was in Templar country. It was on Friday, October 13th, 1307 that the French king made his move against the Templars, massacred hundreds of them, stole what treasures they had not secreted away and brought that noble organisation to an ignominious end.

At 19:30 the restaurant opened. I am starving and Maurinus invites me to join them. There is no sign of the Scottish family returning so I join Maurinus, Susan, Franz (a very funny guy) and Johann. They have been together since St Jean but they accepted me into their group as if they had known me forever. The Spaniard I met in Fromista is here also. As I said he speaks no English but as he always does when we meet, he waves and shouts Hola.

Susan, whose surname is Herlihy but I did not find that out until many months after I got home, must go home tomorrow so a small farewell party is quickly arranged and from what I can gather, she will be badly missed by her group.

Buenos Noches y Buen Camino

To Leon and on to La Virgen del Camino

Day 9, Sunday, 15th September

Today I am taking the train so no big rush to get up and on the road. There are about another 6 or so peregrinos also on board. I am sitting with Michael from Australia who is on his way home. Seems a shame to come all that way and not have enough time to get to Santiago. Also on board is the lady from Leitrim that I first met back in Carrion. Her name is Antoinette. From the station in Leon, after saying goodbye to Michael, it's a straight road up to the Cathedral where Antoinette and I go to misa (mass). After mass, we meet up with some of her other companions who are heading back 2 or 3km along the route to an albergue, and then spend the day sightseeing. Should I join them or walk the few km to Virgen and stay there. Once again I make the right decision and walk on (my guardian angel must be whispering in my ear each time I have a decision to make as it always turns out to be the right one).

The map shows a steep hill up to Virgen but its better behind me than waiting for me first thing in the morning. The walk through Leon is not great. I really do not like pavement pounding. There are three peregrinos ahead of me but they must be walking at the same pace as they never get any further ahead and I don't get any closer. The streets are getting really steep now and I am still in the city; when do I get out into the countryside again and tackle the hill up to Virgen? As I come to the end of the residential area and enter the commercial district it is time for a break. There is a park bench at the corner of a street and a litter bin, a good place to stop. An old man with a walking cane and in his slippers comes along and joins me. He has no English and even though I tell him 'no habla español' he continues to chat away; I think he was just glad of some company. After binning my rubbish I set off up the hill and out onto a busy road. Hooray! I read the map wrong and I am in La Virgen del Camino. It is what we might call a suburb of Leon. It's a pleasant surprise as I thought I still had another hill to contend with.

The albergue is round the back of the café La Peregrino but it is not opened yet. It is in the grounds of a seminary so there is a large lawn to relax on and in the middle of the lawn there is a man sitting all on his own and he tells me that it won't be opened for another 15 minutes or so. From his accent I reckon he may be German or Dutch. He is Mees van der Sluijs and he is from the Netherlands.

This is a very good albergue with a fine cocino (kitchen) and lounge/library/internet café. With the last of my food I throw together a small lunch. Chicken soup followed by tuna, cheese and nuts. Previous pilgrims have left behind some stuff to be used freely so I got a nice bottle of orange, a yoghurt and some coffee. There was some wine but it's a bit early for that. Suppose I should go out and find somewhere to have dinner tonight. The albergue is starting to fill up now but so far there is no-one who wants to mix and chat. French and Germans who tend to keep to themselves and some Canadians. Of the three batches of Canadians I have met, two groups have been more like 'yanks abroad'. No wonder the Canadian lady I met way back at Rabé did not come into the albergue in Castrojeriz when I told her there were some Canadians in. Can't stand them she said and I thought she was joking.

I asked the hospitalero why the town was called La Virgen. With the use of her dictionary we managed to understand what each other was saying. She brought me into the library and got out an old book that told the story in pictures. In 1505, the Blessed Virgin appeared to a shepherd boy and told him to throw a stone and where that stone should fall, a church was to be built. The vision was of the Virgin with the Crucified Christ lying across her knees, Her face almost ugly with the torment of it.

The vision is depicted in the Cathedral in Leon as well as in this local church. In the 19th century, the old church collapsed but the altar was rescued and a new church was built around it.

Over the front façade there are 13 statues, Mary and the twelve apostles. Mary is in the middle hovering higher than the others and at one end is Saint James looking west towards Santiago. I believe she called me here to see this shrine and to pray here. I had thought about staying in Leon but I am so glad I didn't. I wonder what Jesus and his Holy Mother have in store for me tomorrow. Should I take the path to Villar de Mazariffe or the sendo to Villadangos del Paramo? I am sure they will guide me.

After visiting the shrine, it was time for my usual scouting trip. I had read in the Brierley guide about the signage outside of town and reading between the lines he would appear to be disgusted with it. Surely I thought, it can't be as bad as Mr. Brierley says. Well it was worse. Signs pointing every which way and there is no way I could have made sense of them in the dark but I now know which way to go; Villar de Mazariffe it will be. I hope there are no more competing signs further out.

It is now time for dinner. The café Peregrino has a pilgrim menu so I make my way round just in time for the kitchen opening. I am sitting on my own tonight. The meal does not include the usual Tinto but I ask for it anyway and act dumb and it works, the waiter brings me a two glass carafe. I exchange a few words with a man on his own at the next table and he invites me to join him rather than both of us eating alone. He is French and his name is Raoul.

Back to the albergue for bedtime and I exchange a few words with the Dutch guy, Mees. I will meet him again; in fact, he will become an important part of my life

Buenos Noches y Buen Camino

La Virgen to Villar de Mazariffe

Day 10, Monday, 16th September

This morning I have awakened earlier than usual and can't get back to sleep. I might as well get up and on the road. I am up at the café at just after 6. It is not yet open. Let's try the other café at the end of town, not open either, nothing is, so off up the path on an empty stomach but there is a bar in the next town, Fresno del Camino about 2km away.

Everything is fine until I come to a roundabout on a main road. Which way to go? It takes a bit of time to find the yellow arrow in the dark and I am on the verge of sitting down and waiting till someone else comes along or the sun comes up. Once again, I turn to the power of prayer. At the last gasp I find the arrow and head of down the road and under a flyover. I am now well on track for Fresno. Looking at John Brierley's map, I don't think I should have ever come to that roundabout, the whole thing is most confusing. I would like to see this whole mish mash of competing routes sorted out.

Damn it. It's too early and everything here in Fresno is closed too so I will have to settle for a snack from my dwindling supplies and water at a roadside picnic table. Before starting off I switched on the led lights on my hi-viz straps attached to the back of my pack. I only mention this as it will prove significant later on.

It is only two kilometres to the next village, Oncina, but there are no arrows to tell me I am on the right road so it seems so much longer. I am about to start retracing my steps when I spot a light in the distance and decide to carry on to that point before making a decision. Just outside the village there is a large Camino sign and a fountain so I have been on the right road after all. I look around and see two pilgrims coming towards me, Mees and Raoul who were also unsure of their way in the dark so had been following the lights I had switched on. Raoul is in a hurry as he does not want to stop in Mazariffe as he stayed there last time he was here so wants to go further and stay in a new place. Mees on the other hand does not appear to be in any kind of rush so stops to talk and walks for a little way with me before moving on as I walk too slow. I did not know it at the time, but to quote the final phrase from the Humphrey Bogart movie, 'Casablanca', 'this could be the start of a beautiful friendship'.

[108]

At last I am off the road and on to a gently undulating dusty trail. This is where I see a strange thing for the first time. Peregrinos who have made it to Santiago are walking back along the trail on their way home. When you think about it, this is the traditional way. There were no aeroplanes for the medieval pilgrim and the only way home was the same way they got there; our modern pilgrimage is so much easier.

Eventually I come across a number of women obviously out for a stroll so I know I must be close to another village, Chozas de Abajo. Slightly off the track there is a bar and restaurant and the owner has painted yellow arrows with the word bar but he provides more arrows to take the pilgrim back to the Camino. Sitting on the porch enjoying his coffee Americano is Mees. By the time I get mine and a bite to eat he is ready to move on so we agree to meet in Mazariffe. While I am eating, Antoinette whom I left in Leon arrives and joins me. She took a local bus from Leon to Virgen before walking again. We walk together for the next 4.5km to Mazariffe. Along the way she sees a small dead owl and to my surprise, she picks it up and examines it. It only had one talon but did it lose it before or after it died. Antoinette realises what she has done and drops the bird, then helps herself to some anti-septic gel I keep hanging from my hiking vest. We arrive in Mazariffe but Antoinette does not stop at the albergue and heads on, Mees, on the other hand, is waiting at the gate for me and we go in together. I will not meet Antoinette again.

Once settled in I head down the hill into town to find a store to buy some food for the next day's walk. I find a Spar, wow, I thought they were only in Ireland and Britain. As I come out I miss my turn and head of up the wrong road. What a laugh, I have walked all this way and get lost going to the shop. Fortunately, an old man spots me and realises I am a peregrino so shouts after me and points me to the albergue which is to the right and I was about to turn left.

Back at the albergue, everyone is enjoying a relaxing afternoon in the sun on the front lawn on garden recliners. Some Irish arrive by taxi claiming they went the other option by mistake and have planned to meet friends here. One girl starts talking about her medical history and I get around to telling her about my paralysis, Guillen Barré syndrome, back in the 70s. Surprisingly she knows about it. Another Irish girl chips in to ask if she heard me right. She is a nurse and also knows about it. In the 42 years since I had that, I have never met anyone who had ever heard of it and here I am in a garden in Spain meeting two people inside 5 minutes who are both aware of it.

This albergue, San Antonio Padua, is run by a man known as Pepe. He is famous for his massages as he is a qualified physiotherapist and just as famous for his paella so obviously we are all looking forward to dinner. One of the Irish arrives back in the garden and declares they will not find any cordon bleu dining in this town. I thought he was joking but apparently he was dead serious and rather than join the rest of us for dinner they ordered a taxi and took off for some other eatery.

At dinner Mees and I are sitting together and getting to know each other a little better. Two Americans who are ok but can't leave their anti-Obama republican politics at home become quite annoying so Mees gets up and leaves without a word. I left shortly after and the Americans went into a private room. Maybe they got the idea that we were not interested in their politics as we met them on another couple of occasions along the way and they were much easier to get on with as no politics were mentioned. It's time to hit the hay but at least it's with the confidence that Pepe is providing a good breakfast in the morning

Buenos Noches y Buen Camino

Mazariffe to Hospital de Orbigo

Day 11, Tuesday, 17th September

Today is a short day. Mees has a schedule planned that will get him to Santiago on the 3rd of October as he has a ticket for a bus home on the 5th. He is taking a bus home from Santiago to the Netherlands, that's some journey but that's for another day. We are planning on 15km today, then it is just 279 still to go; it doesn't sound too far if you say it quickly and don't you love my use of the word 'just'. If I can stick to between 16 and 20km a day from here on in I should make it on schedule. Trouble is, today and tomorrow sees the last of the flat walking and its back into the mountains for the rest of the Camino.

I have started out on my own in the dark but a short distance later before even getting out of town Mees catches up with an Austrian girl who has asked to walk with us until it gets light. She is afraid of walking in the dark alone, an unfounded fear, but it is easier to enjoy her company than try to convince her she is as safe as can be.

As the sky starts to brighten, I have a minor accident that I think nothing of but it will come back to plague me later. We are walking on a tarmac road and the edges are a bit the worse for wear. I have taken my eyes off the road and step on a bad portion and go over on my left ankle. It is not too sore and I assume my good hiking boots have protected me. I think no more of it and after a short distance the pain goes away.

We are walking along country lanes now and Mees says he wants to push on and will meet me in Hospital de Orbigo. The Austrian girl has long since gone on her way. At a crossroad outside Milla del Páramo I find Mees having a snack on a park bench. He is just about to leave so once again we take our leave of each other. At last I reach the outskirts of Hospital and to my dismay, I find more of the practice of painting out arrows to send pilgrims towards a destination not of their choosing. I have just crossed a flyover on the A-71 and it is not clear if I should cross the road to my left and into a field or keep on straight. Some pilgrims are heading straight on so I follow. What this does is take me onto the path from yesterday's option to Villadangos but at least there are now yellow arrows to comfort me. As I walk down towards the river I spot a bar to the right and who should be enjoying his coffee but my friend Mees. Seems like a good place to rest for a while and neither of

[111]

us is in any hurry to move on. Seems he came up the street from the opposite direction to this bar so he turned left at the bottom of the flyover.

Spanning the river and a wide plain that at one time was a much wider river is one of the longest medieval bridges in Spain. According to Brierley, it dates from the 13th century and was built over an earlier Roman bridge. It seems that in the Holy Year of 1434 there was a jousting tournament here and the bridge is known as Paso Honroso, the passage of honour. It was also the scene of a battle between the Moors and the forces of Alfonso III. The village on the other side, Hospital de Orbigo gets its name from the Knights of the Order of St John who maintained a pilgrim hospital here and of course Orbigo from the river.

We booked into the albergue San Miguel which was highly recommended in Mees's Dutch guide book. It is also an artists gallery and there is a canvas and paints set aside for any pilgrim who fancies trying their hand at painting. Once we are settled I go for a walk around town. I am all out of Vaseline for my feet and I lost Christopher's foot

My Friend Mees

balm a long way back at Hornillos on the Meseta. I eventually find a Farmacia and get something that will do for now but I must find somewhere that sells that foot balm. On the way back I bump into Mees who has also been out exploring and off we go together. We find a very unusual house, a new build with solar panels on the roof but it is designed like a castle with turrets.

I am feeling really good today. I check my blood glucose and it's down to 4.7. I am feeling so good I start to allow myself to

[112]

believe I am going to make it all the way. Mees has met another Dutch guy so I head out to dinner on my own and leave them to chat in their own language. I found a really good restaurant and had a good meal with a number of other pilgrims, one an Irish man called Val. Halfway through the meal Mees arrived and we eventually made our way back to the albergue together.

Tomorrow there is an option at the end of the town. Straight on takes you over some trail to a sendo which follows the N-120 to Astorga. The other option which turns right at the end of town is all trails but it is over a 900m hill so I reckon with the amount of hills coming up over the next week, I will avoid this one. Mees is for going over the hill so we agree to meet up tonight in Santa Catalina de Somoza on the other side of Astorga.

Buenos Noches y Buen Camino

Hospital to Murias de Rechivaldo

Day 12, Wednesday, 18th September

It is an early start today. The artist who runs this place is providing breakfast and what do you know, real toast for a change. Tostada in Spain is usually one of their very hard bread rolls very lightly toasted with butter and apricot jam. Strangely, in the country that gave us Seville oranges, marmalade seems to be unknown.

There is no point waiting for Mees today as he is taking the other option at the top of the town so it's out into the cold dark morning about 6:40 on my own. At the end of town where the options diverge, in the blackness of fields and sky there is an amazing moon hanging like a lantern in the blackness of space. Just below it is a street light so in the darkness, I can see two globes of light and nothing else.

There is nothing much to see this morning, just try to follow the trail in the pitch black. In the distance I can see road lights and eventually traffic starts to appear on the road but it's a lonely walk as there is no-one else out yet. Eventually the trail becomes a sendo along the N120. I am walking on what appears to be an old road that has been replaced by the modern highway running parallel to it. To my left there are vineyards and every now and then along the way, small makeshift seats have been set up and bunches of grapes left on them for the passing peregrino. I stop at one for a snack and to rest my left foot, which if you remember, I twisted yesterday on the way out of Mazariffe and its starting to bother me again. Hopefully I will be able to walk it off as the day goes on. I certainly hope so as I have planned a 26km day today and Mees and I will meet up in Santa Catalina on the other side of Astorga tonight. Coincidently as I think about Mees, I hear a voice behind me ask *'Is this the way to Santiago'*. It's Mees. He had started out with two French guys and at the top of the town had walked straight ahead with them and ended up taking the same option that I had.

Together Mees and I walk together and continue to get to know each other and form a friendship that will last beyond the Camino.

The trail now crosses the road and climbs up to the Cruceiro de Santo Toribio. Just below the cross is a viewpoint with a map of

[114]

the Astorga region. There is also a busker playing the guitar and wishing everyone Buen Camino. From here we can see Astorga laid out before us and beyond the city we can see the Montes de Léon. We must cross these mountains in the next few days but for today, it's just the heat to worry about; it is not yet lunch time and already it is pretty hot. A short distance further on we arrive in the outskirts of Astorga, a village called San Justo de la Vega where we stop for a coffee at the first café we come to. Mees tells me that he wants to push on a little faster and will meet me tonight so he sets off down the hill at his own pace and eventually, as I pass through a commercial district, I lose sight of him ahead. There is a tall footbridge to negotiate to get over the railway tracks (makes a heck of a racket, iron bridge and walking poles) and a lot of crossings over the roads that encircle the town but eventually I am in the old town and boy, it is one steep climb up to the city centre and by the time I make it to Plaza San Francisco I am completely shattered. There is a nice café in the corner of the plaza so I reckon this is a good time for lunch. The waitress has a look at my map and points me in the right direction and I set off

towards Catedral St Marta in Plaza Catedral. Also in the plaza is the Palacio Episcopal (Bishop's palace) designed by Gaudi who designed the Sacra Familia in Barcelona. There is a vintage car rally outside the Palacio so I stop to take a couple of pics before heading on and walking straight into a large funeral.

As I continue out of town, the pain in my foot is not getting any better; in fact it is quite a bit worse. As I leave town there is a park so I sit down on a bench to try relacing my boot to see if it will ease the pain. I still have 9km to go to Santa Catalina but at the minute I have my doubts about reaching the other side of the park but I have no option but to keep walking. Once again I ask my walking companion, Jesus, to get behind me and push. How do people with no faith in anything manage to get by? Without faith, there have been a number of times that I would have given up. According to the map there is an albergue a short distance away but it's well short of Santa Catalina. At the road junction where I would need to turn for the albergue, there is an old hermitage, all that remains of a pilgrim hospice, Ecce Homo. Should I turn right up to the modern albergue or push on over the motorway flyover. After a short rest in the hermitage, I filled my bottles from the fuenta and, feeling somewhat refreshed, but still in pain, I opt for pushing on; I really must reach Santa Catalina tonight. However, as I reach Murias I must concede defeat. My left instep is really sore now so I will have to stop in the albergue here and resign myself to the fact I will not see Mees again. I ask two other pilgrims who are heading on to ask for him and tell him I will try to catch up later. Doubt they will find him but who knows.

Dinner is part of the service here but as the weather is good, the hospitalero brings the tables out from the kitchen and we eat al fresco. There is a group of Irishmen at the table who have been together since Saint Jean Pied de Port. One of them is a rugby coach from Mayo and the other is from Dublin. This coming Sunday is the All Ireland football final and guess which two teams are contesting it, Mayo and Dublin. In true Irish fashion the craic is as they say, 90. They tell me that there is a café back down the road a little that is serving breakfast from six so I will not be walking hungry in the morning. They refer to it as first breakfast and are planning second breakfast in Santa Catalina and then third breakfast at the next place that's open. These guys are mad.

An early night is needed tonight. Tomorrow is going to be tough. It is all uphill to Santa Catalina, flat to El Ganso then uphill again to Rabanal. It is only 16km to Rabanal and then another 5 to Foncebaden. Not sure which one I will stop in. Foncebaden would be good so that next day I could be up at La Cruz de Ferro before dawn and sit and watch the sun rise. This is the highest point of the whole trek. It is just a simple iron cross on top of a huge pole but for centuries, peregrinos have been leaving a stone at the base, a stone they have carried from home. Some say it represents a token of love and blessing, others say it represents the unburdening of all your problems. I think it is just a nice traditional gesture that is very old. The origins I will go into later but for now

Buenos Noches y Buen Camino

Murias to Rabanal

Day 13, Thursday, 19th September

Another dark morning to start walking but at least I am having breakfast with my Irish friends from last night. They were up before me so finish eating before I am ready to leave. As I start out I realise I have left my knife and torch in the albergue so I leave my friends to walk on while I go to look for it. When I come back out I can just about discern there lights disappearing into the distance. Oh well, walking on my own again but it's not so bad. It gives me time to say my morning prayers as I walk and just let my thoughts wander where they will. I start each day with the Morning Offering, the prayer to my Guardian Angel and the prayer to Our Lady associated with the Miraculous Medal that I wear all the time along with the one I was given back in Rabé.

At last I reach Santa Catalina where I should have been with Mees last night. He was a lovely guy and a great companion. I will miss him a lot. Unfortunately when you walk as slowly as I do, it is just a natural occurrence along the Camino, make friends for a few hours then probably never see them again. Maybe some of them will still be in Santiago if and when I finally get there.

In the meantime, I spot the lights of another café up ahead. Second breakfast I laugh. There at the table are the Irish guys enjoying a coffee. After a short chat they are on their way again and I finish my coffee alone. They say they might stay an extra night in Ponferrada if they can find somewhere to watch the game so I think maybe I will meet them again, alas, I never will.

I must be getting fitter as the hill up to here did not drain me as other hills have. Anyway it is fairly flat to El Ganso and an uneventful hike.

I have forgotten to replenish my water supplies and I have not come across any fountains today so I hope there is somewhere in this village. This is the first in a number of semi abandoned villages in these mountains, the others being Foncebaden, Manjarin, El Acebo and Riego de Ambróse. In this little place however there is a seemingly well-known watering hole, the Cowboy Bar. I wonder will they fill my bottles for me, suppose they can only say no so I enter through the beaded curtains, show my water bottle and say in a questioning tone, *'agua'*. It works and the lady kindly fills my bottle and I am on my way again.

The hill is not as steep as this morning but it is long and constant and my foot is starting to hurt again, not as bad as yesterday but it is slowing me down and consequently, it takes me a total of 5 hours to finally reach Rabanal. That's just about 3km/ hour and that's not good enough, I really need to be doing at least 4. At the first café/bar I come to, I stop for lunch. Its only noon so I think maybe I should push on to Foncebaden since it is only 5km but pretty steep. Unfortunately, having sat in the sun enjoying coffee and a snack for too long, I have lost the will to get up and go so I book into the albergue next door to the bar, means I won't have to go far for dinner tonight.

It is time to take a long hard look at my pilgrim's progress. I have ten days of September left and 150 miles still to go. (Still can't get used to thinking in kilometres). At my current pace, I will still be 50 miles short of Santiago at the turn of the month and that's leaving it tight if I want to fly home on October 5th. On top of everything I have fallen behind everyone I have met. Oh well, c'est la vie.

I take my usual walk to the other end of town to see if there are any complications in the route that may be hard to follow in the dark but it is very straight forward. On the way back down, I spot a sign for Pizza, what the heck; I shall treat myself to a little rest and relaxation with a pizza and a cold beer. The sheer decadence of it.

Back in the albergue I meet another Irishman. His name is Jack and he is good friends with Ed and Ger whom I had dinner with last night. I briefly met a couple from Musgrave Park in Belfast whose daughter lives close to us in Glengormley. Nicole, whom I met back in Boadilla has also turned up as has Nadje from I think Hungary but I am not sure. I think she was the girl Mees and I walked out of Mazariffe with although at the time I thought she was Austrian. I thought I was alone here in Rabanal but as it turns out, you are never alone out here. You may be walking on your own at times but you are never alone.

It is like old times back in Belfast here. A damned helicopter keeps flying overhead. I forgot to mention, that on the way into Rabanal there was a large house with a copter parked in the front garden. I hope he does not keep this up all night. It's the one sound I don't like at night. It generally meant the Brits were out raiding back in the decades of our war and often resulted in something bad happening. I don't think I will ever get used to the noise of that contraption.

Its dinner time so Jack and I head next door for a pleasant meal and a long chat before hitting the hay. Jack says he will have to motor on tomorrow as he wants to catch up with his friends. Another dinner companion that I will never meet again

Buenos Noches y Buen Camino

Rabanal to El Acebo

Day 14, Friday 20th September

It's not a bad morning and the climb up to Foncebaden was easier than I had expected. I walk part of the way with a young Englishman but I didn't get his name. He was not into the café con leche way of life so he heads on while I stop in Foncebaden for a short break before the ascent up to La Cruz de Ferro.

The Cruz is a bit disappointing. There is a bit of a tourist attraction kind of atmosphere about it. Some find it a very soothing place and take some quiet time up by the old stone chapel for peaceful reflection but I get the impression that most people are stopping here for the proverbial photo opportunity because they think they have to, having read about it or seen it in the Martin Sheen movie, 'The Way.' By the way, mention of this movie has come up many times along the way and it's amazing how many folk actually think it's a true story. It is a very good movie, but pure fiction taken from a number of short stories about the camino.

But anyway, more about this cross. How long has it been here, who put it here and why? One theory is that it is merely a marker to indicate the position of the road as it frequently disappears when it snows. In fact, along the road there are tall marker poles to indicate the path of the road when there is heavy snow. Another is that it was just a pile of stones called Montes de Mercurio, in honour of the god Mercury, that once again marked the road and has been here since Celtic times and later a cross was added by a local abbot called Gaucelmo when Spain became Christian. When the name, La Cruz de Ferro, was added I do not know. Either way, for me the place was nothing more than a picnic site and did nothing for me. After a snack and some water, I headed off down the hill and never looked back. I did concede to tradition however and left a stone that I had carried from Ireland.

The descent down to Manjarin, where there is a famous road
sign pointing the way to the four corners of the globe, is steep
but not too difficult. Funny saying that as a globe doesn't have
any corners let alone four. The trail now leaves the road and
winds its way along the side of the mountain through ferns and
undergrowth as green as Ireland. It skirts just below Punto Alto
which is slightly higher than the Cruz but thankfully it doesn't
climb up to the summit. It's now downhill to El Acebo which is
about 400m lower down the mountain. Now, you might think
reading this that 'whoopee,' it's downhill. Don't be fooled. This
downhill is worse than any climb on the Camino. It is steep,
dusty and rocky, a mountain goat trail that even the goats don't
use. Some people are actually running down but if they lose
their footing at speed, they will do a lot of damage. Didn't their
daddies tell them to never run down a hill I think to myself. The
picture of my daughter Nicola ignoring this advice and bouncing
along on her chin springs to mind. This is where my son,
Christopher fell last year and badly cut his hand. Another inch
he says and he would have been using his nose for a brake.
Tomorrow in Ponferrada I will see a woman who did just that
and her face looked like she had just gone three rounds with
the heavyweight champion of the world. But for now, this is
sheer torture. It's getting really hot and the path is so steep I
can't make any speed on it. I can feel myself getting
dehydrated no matter how much I drink. At one rest point I am
overtaken by an American man and his son. I have been having
problems with my camera all day and am sitting fiddling with it
trying to get it to switch on long enough to take a picture. The
son stops to talk and shows me his rubberised shock proof, idiot
proof (his words) camera before heading on. A short while later
I pass him as he has stopped for a cigarette and he tells me
that he just has to have one otherwise he will become grumpy.
As we meet a few more times over the coming days, I take to

calling him Grumpy and he just calls me Irish. I grew to like these two Americans a lot.

At last, I stumble into El Acebo and seek out the first albergue I can. Seems there are four and I missed the first one which was fortunate as I found a great one upstairs in the local bar. Hopefully I will feel better after a shower as I am feeling very low at the minute but the shower does not help, I even feel slightly sick. As I sit on the side of my bed feeling really miserable, Nicole turns up again and asks, with a little concern in her voice, if I am OK. She says I look really awful and reckons I am badly dehydrated. She calls over another Dutch friend she has been walking with. I can't recall his name but he is wearing a tee shirt the same as the one Mees has but that's a story I will find out about another day. In the meantime, Nicole explains that he had also been very ill with dehydration and had to spend a night in hospital so she asks him for one of the rehydration powders the hospital gave him and she mixes it up with some water for me. Whatever it was, it worked almost instantly and I was able to enjoy the rest of the day relaxing in the back beer garden of the bar with Nicole and her friend and a cold beer or two. Why is it that when I am at my lowest, someone turns up and with a simple act of Christian charity, lifts my spirits again? Just as dinner time was coming around I discovered that Jolly, the American girl I had met back in Calzadilla was also in the albergue.

It's a funny thing but I just don't remember having dinner that night or who I had it with. One of the few blank spots of my camino.

As I mentioned back in Uterga, I had hoped I would never suffer a day like that again but today was just as bad and amazingly the thing that really drained me on both days was the downhill section, not the climb. Will there be any more days like this. I hope not but for now, I need sleep so

Buenos Noches y Buen Camino

El Acebo to Ponferrada

Day 15, Saturday, 21st September

Today I am two weeks on the camino from Burgos to Ponferrada. At Burgos I had 501km to walk to Santiago. Today I have 206.4km to go so I have 294.6km behind me, an average of around 20.8km per day. (Using kilometres now instead of miles because the conversion process was really doing my head in). Having almost 300km behind me cheers me up. If anyone had told me before I retired I would walk 20km I would have laughed at them but to walk nearly 300 over all kinds of terrain was beyond my wildest dreams. Over this past two weeks I have found a faith in myself but more importantly, I have found a new faith in Jesus. The old poem you see so often hanging on walls in many homes entitled '*Footprints*' has actually become a real life daily experience. Jesus, his Holy Mother and my Guardian Angel have become very real entities to me that I can talk to like they were visibly beside me. Anyway, morning prayers are said as I walk up the dark street of this village. It is very black as there is virtually no street lighting and, I must admit to being very apprehensive this morning, in fact I mean just plain scared. Although the profile map shows the trail to be a little less steep than yesterday, I will be doing it in the pitch black with just my head torch to guide me. I wonder should I stick to the road today?

As I leave the town I spot a woman looking at road signs and obviously not sure of which way to go but as I had already scouted out the route the night before, I knew which way so I call her and point to the yellow arrow on the road. She joins me and walks with me and as we go she tells me her name is Lynne and she is from New Zealand. I confide in her how frightened I am of this morning's descent on paths that are treacherous enough in daylight but almost impossible in the dark. As we reach the point where the trail leaves the road she says she is going to try it so I tag along. The path down to Riego is, as I had guessed almost impassable, even in the town the road is a broken up rough track. As Lynne walks in front of me I can't help noticing how muscular her legs are. This lady is obviously a very experienced walker and could leave me in her wake without any effort. She is, without any doubt in my mind, holding back to stay with me and guide me down this mountain and I am convinced that God has arranged for us to meet and has provided me with a real life Guardian Angel.

As the sun starts to warm the morning air we arrive in Molinaseca and find a café to have some breakfast. The place is full of Peregrinos including my American friend, Grumpy. A few minutes after we arrived, Nicole also arrived. There was definitely no sign of anyone behind us on the trail on the way down and we did stop a few times to admire the scenery in the early morning light so I wonder is Nicole using taxis now and then. Anyway, Lynne is ready to move on but I still have a freshly squeezed orange to drink and tablets to take so she says if I don't mind, she will press on to Ponferrada and maybe meet me there later. Nicole also leaves before me. I never did learn how to pronounce the Spanish for orange, naranja.

As I make my way out of town I see Nicole and some guy sitting on a wall and she says she is waiting for a taxi. I never saw her again. It's only about 7km to Ponferrada but it is getting pretty hot and its virtually all pavement bashing. There is only one albergue in town and I wish I had studied my map a bit closer as there is an option to follow the road straight into town passing the front door of the albergue, San Nicolas de Flúe. As it is, I follow the yellow arrows that bring me around the outside of town and into the centre a good bit past the albergue. Along this part of the trail I am passed by a couple that I had met back in Calzadilla and had assumed to be German but they are actually Swedish; I never got their names but they just called me the 'Irish Guy'. They tell me they are not stopping here but I met them later that day so they must have changed their minds

At last, I turn into the courtyard of the albergue and there are a few rucksacks lying about and a couple of peregrinos who tell me it won't be opened until 2pm, Oh well, just have to wait. There is a familiar looking rucksack lying beside a bench. Where have I seen it before? At that point, I hear my name being called and look up to see Mees come across the path towards me, I knew I recognised that backpack. He seems as pleased to see me as I am of him. Maurinus whom I met in Sahagún is also here and later Franz and Johann also turn up as does Nadje and Jolly and my Swedish friends. Then I make a big mistake. My boots are covered in the yellowish dust of the mountains so I get the Nikwax out and proceed to clean them. Mees finds this hilarious, a pilgrim cleaning his boots, so he takes a picture of me and threatens to put it on the internet when he gets home and he did too. I will never live that one down.

It's not an unpleasant wait in the porch of this albergue. The company is good and the 'craic' is mighty although since I am the only Irish in the company, the rest of them don't know the 'craic' is mighty. That's my little secret. Someone has turned on the fountain in the front porch and it helps to cool the  air. At last the doors open and somehow I find myself at the top of the queue where I should not be but when I try to move back, the pilgrims behind who should have been in front tell me to stay there. Plenty of beds here they say so we will all be accommodated. Unfortunately it means that I am in a different room from Mees and I did want to catch up on our experiences over the last few days. Anyhow, Mees always takes an afternoon nap so I head out to explore the town. The first thing I see is a sign for McDonald's that is pointing down towards the centre of town. Normally I don't particularly like their excuse for burgers but today I really fancy one so off I go in search of Ronald McDonald. I am right into the centre of town but there are no more signs so I give up and head back or at least I thought I was heading back. At a large roundabout I take a wrong turning and am actually heading away from the albergue. When I see the railway tracks in front of me I can confirm what I had been thinking for a few minutes now, I am lost. Three hundred miles across Spain and I get lost on a roundabout, again. But once again Divine Providence comes to my aid when I stop a family to ask for directions. I just happened to pick a family that not only speak good English but know exactly where the albergue is and I am quickly back on the right road after many 'Muchas Gracias'.

Nadje has invited me to join her for dinner that she is preparing in the kitchen. I had found a note on my bed back in Rabanal from some female inviting me to phone her about having dinner together but I had ignored it as I did not know who it was but today I discover that it was Nadje, so this time, I accept her invitation. All she asks is that I provide the wine. Assuming that she plans dinner about 7pm I stop in a little bistro and order some pizza. My Swedish friends are there ordering ice cream and the background music is Irish, the Celtic Legends cd. Shortly after I arrive back in the albergue I realise that Nadje is having dinner a lot earlier than I thought so after asking Mees where he got his supplies I head off to get that wine. In the supermercado I spot tins of Guinness so I just have to buy one. It goes straight into the freezer along with the wine as soon as I get back and shortly thereafter Nadje starts to serve dinner. It is a vegetarian meal and the soup to start is delicious. However the amount of food she has prepared is just too much, especially after that pizza but I try to eat as much as I can. The wine goes down well but that Guinness was the vilest drink I ever tasted. As I write this some eight months after returning home I can still taste that awful brew.

Later in the evening Mees decides to go get some cash so I go with him to show him where the ATM is and we then do some shopping for tomorrow and drop into a local café/bar for coffee and a chat. Although he has already phoned ahead for a bed in Villafranca del Bierzo he decides to join me when I tell him I am getting a bus in the morning to Villafranca and then walking on to Trabadelo. Another good decision as we will find out in a couple of days.

Back at the albergue I get a text message from my travel agent friend, Bruce, with some flight details home on the 5th October. Still plenty of seats left but the fare has gone up but I had expected that as it got closer to the date.

The hospitaleros are turning the common room into a dorm of sorts and putting mattresses outside in the large covered front porch. The large queue of pilgrims who were too late to get a bed are going to get somewhere to lay their heads. Seems this is a regular occurrence here. As there is a spare bed in my room I let them know and a lucky young man gets brought in from the common room floor to a comfortable bed so with my good deed done for the day, it's time to hit the hay

Buenos Noches y Buen Camino

Ponferrada to Trabadelo

Day 16, Sunday, 22nd September

Up early this morning and into the bar before 6:30 to beat the rush. Mees joins me and we relax with our coffees before heading round to the bus station to check the times of the next bus to Villafranca. As we leave the bar and head down the road we are talking and laughing. Just then, a lone pilgrim in front turns and tells us, quite rudely, to be quiet as people are sleeping. It's not a request, it's an order. I am about to lose my cool when Mees puts his hand on my shoulder and calms me down. This is the first nasty pilgrim I have met, in fact, thankfully, he is the only one but I suppose it takes all kinds to make a pilgrimage.

We have a bit of a wait at the bus station. Seems busses don't start as early as pilgrims, especially on a Sunday. By the way, the toilets in the Ponferrada estacion de autobus leave an awful lot to be desired. We board at 9am and are in Villafranca by 9:30am. The bus drops us at a little hotel on the edge of town so that's a cue for second breakfast. There is no point in stopping here, a total waste of a day if we do, so I suggest we get a few km in to shorten tomorrows walk so we set of for Trabadelo. There are two routes to choose from, the sendo along the N-IV or the Camino Durro climbing steeply to Alto Pradela. The N-IV is the road mentioned by Hape Kerkeling in his book, '*I'm Off Then*'. It is no longer as dangerous as he relates since the new A6 motorway opened and took away most of the traffic. Also, there is now a dedicated sendo with concrete barriers separating it from the road. After the last few days I have had my fill of mountains and with O'Cebreiro ahead, the steepest climb on the Way, the sendo seems the best bet.

After an uneventful walk, mostly uphill but fairly gradual, we arrive in Trabadelo at noon. We pay an extra €2 for a room with just 6 beds, no bunks and a private bathroom. We got some washing done and as we were first in there is lots of room on the clothes line on the rooftop patio. It's as hot as Hades out there today so the clothes should dry quickly. I find a shady corner and decide to phone Margaret for a bit of a chat and she tells me there is a problem with Sarah's car, something about the brakes.

[127]

Back in the dorm a Dutch couple has arrived and a couple of women from where, I do not know, for, as they did not engage in conversation I found out nothing about them other than what my eyes told me. One of them is getting cream put on as she is covered in bites, bedbug bites. The Dutch couple are spraying their beds with all sorts of stuff. Do they know something I do not? Later I ask them and they tell me they have been having problems with bed bugs all along the Camino. The man has found one in his bed so I start to take my bed apart to make sure I have none. They report it to the hospitalero and she comes up immediately to investigate and she helps me to check my bed but Mees, I nor any of the others find anything in our beds. The Hospitalero invites us all to move to another room which she double checks before we settle in, she intends to fumigate the room we are evacuating. The Dutch couple decide to get a refund and move on. By this time the old man with the donkey has also joined us and his bed is clear too. We all come to the conclusion that the Dutch couple have picked them up somewhere and are carrying them in their backpack, a not uncommon occurrence with these little monsters.

Another great dinner tonight and back to bed and hopefully no bugs. Tomorrow the climbing starts in earnest. By the way, I found a little shop at the top of the town that sold the foot balm that I lost way back in Hornillos. It is good stuff, quite expensive but well worth it

Buenos Noches y Buen Camino

Trabadelo to La Faba

Day 17, Monday 23rd September

Today Mees has planned a shorter day so that the steep climb is split in two and, with hindsight, it was a very good idea.

There is no breakfast to be had in this town so it's hit the road with just a drink of water. It's a little confusing as we go through some underpasses at the motorway and the way is not well marked but we do find our way out of the little maze of trails and bridges. Along the sendo we come to a huge truck stop, café and hotel, Breakfast Time!! Not actually sure in the dark, where we are but I think it is La Portela de Valcarce. Breakfast is great, the best toast I have had since arriving in Spain; it's made with olive oil. There is an ATM here so I decide to withdraw another €50 for no other reason than to find out how much I have left. Unfortunately it cannot give me a balance on a prepaid card so I am none the wiser but a short time later the card provider sends a txt alert to say I have €138 left. That's great, more than I thought I had.

As we walk on towards Herrerías, the last town before the climb starts, I get a message from my daughter, Cathy, to tell me she has passed her driving theory test. Well done girl.

I keep waiting for the trail to start climbing steeply but it is still a gradual slope. Along the way we see a sign offering horses to O' Cebreiro. What a time to learn how to ride a horse, I think I will pass on this one. Mees has moved well ahead of me because I stopped to take some pictures and then found I could not catch up but no matter, we are staying in an agreed albergue so I will see him later, well, I have to as there is nowhere else to stop. I round a small bend in the road and there he is sitting on a crash barrier waiting for me. After a little rest and snack we head on and at last come to a sign that says La Faba, on schedule, just where we planned to be at 11am.

Off we go and slowly but surely I am falling behind until Mees is well out of sight. It is only 3k up to the albergue but it feels like

I have been walking forever. The trail is nothing more than another of those goat trails. All morning we have been hearing cowbells in the fields but now I hear them much closer. I am on my own now, not another pilgrim in sight and there is a herd of cows coming down the trail straight at me. These are not like Irish cows, they are more akin to the longhorns you would see in a western movie. One cow has a deep bloody gash in its side presumably from one of these sharp horns. Once again, Jesus, Mary and my Guardian Angel are called upon for help. They must have heard me because as I stand there like a statue the cows pass on either side of me with nothing more than a gentle bump or two. I am walking and climbing again but only just. This is really tough and lying down and dying seems like a good option. My whole being is screaming at me to stop but I know that if I do, I won't get started again. Just then I hear a friendly voice and a hand on my shoulder. It is Lynne who led me down from El Acebo. She asks if I am OK and tells me, *"Keep hydrated Terry, keep hydrated"* before she storms on up the hill. Her very presence is enough to give me that extra little push. Jesus has sent help to me again. Unfortunately, I will never see Lynne again; I really liked that lady. This climb is taking about 45 minutes and as I found out later, most others did it in 20 to 25 minutes. That 45 minutes by the way felt like hours.

How much further do I have to go? Is it just around the next bend? Please God let it be the next bend. As I turn the next bend I hear a voice shouting, *"push Terry, push"*. I look up and there is Mees standing at a parapet without his rucksack. Nearly there he shouts. Well it is but it's still steep and rough and by the time I get up to him I am almost bent double with only my walking poles keeping me up.

This albergue, by an old church does not open until 2pm so we have quite a wait so I dump my pack beside some others which turns out to be the start of a queue of packs. A cheerful group now congregate around the fountain in the courtyard and start bathing their feet in it. The atmosphere has turned very cheerful and pilgrims are coming and going, some are adding their packs to the queue and others after a rest and a chat move on. Some of those staying head into the town in search of refreshments but Mees and I have enough left over from our last shopping trip so we just relax under a tree and eat the last of our food. At last the hospitalero arrives and is amazed at the orderly queue; she has never seen this before, so rather than

[130]

starting to let us in she goes off to get her camera to record the event for posterity.

Eventually she starts admissions. She only lets 2 or 3 in at a time so that her colleague can bring each group in and assign them a bed. I hear a voice behind me telling everyone where they should be in the queue. It's the nasty guy from Ponferrada and he sets himself up at an empty desk and starts telling everyone who is next and people are listening to him. Who appointed him the camino policeman? I am having none of this. This guy would not last ten minutes in Belfast, a right wee Adolf. He points to someone behind me and calls them forward, screw this, I walk up to the desk even though he tries to tell me it's not my turn. I give him my best dirty look and walk on. I am shown to my bed, a bottom bunk and another guy is in the bottom bunk beside me. Who should come in next but the nasty guy and he gets the bunk above me. He wants one of us to give up our bed as he has a wee problem and has to get up for the bathroom at night, don't we all. Into the top bunk with you, nobody is buying your grief. Hope no-one snores he declares, well I do and tonight I will start before I go to sleep. Is this the way a pilgrim should be thinking and behaving I think to myself? Probably not but I can't help myself with this rather obnoxious guy. Later I do relent and pray that he found some kind of peace of mind on the Camino. After today I never met him again.

Just down the dorm I hear an American voice that sounds familiar. It's Jolly. She has a bed but her bags are outside. She is such a nice young girl. She tells me that no-one who stayed in the albergue in Villafranca was allowed in until their sleeping bags had been thoroughly checked and sprayed with insecticide. Seems the albergue had bedbugs some weeks ago and this hospitalero is taking no chances. The decision to walk on past Villafranca was as I said earlier, the right one without knowing it.

A few days ago in El Acebo, I met an Englishman called Chris. Now, if snoring was an Olympic event, this guy would win gold. He is even worse than Phil from Galway who could snore for Ireland. That's the background to the next story. Mees and I have made our way round to the café and have got a table out under a canopy. Across the table there are two people but I don't look up to see who it is as my phone rings. Its Margaret to tell me that Sarah's car is not as bad as they first thought. Well, because she is always going on about me snoring I just have to tell her about Chris. At that moment, I look up and the person at the other side of the table is, you guessed it, Chris. He is having a great laugh and so is Margaret on the other end of the phone while I am slightly embarrassed. Another drink all round and then the taxi Chris has been waiting for arrives to take him and his girl to O'Cebreiro. Goodbye Chris, it was fun. I never met him again or heard him snore.

Another great dinner tonight, fried eggs and bacon, just like home and it takes my mind of tomorrow's climb. I have contacted my son Chris to ask him about the next section and he says that the next stretch is tough but not as bad as the climb I made today. Hope he is right but only tomorrow will tell. For now, all I can say is I have had three extremely tough days, more so than any other. Mount Perdon on my first day, the descent to El Acebo three days ago and the climb today to La Faba. Hopefully now, I have conquered the toughest sections and from here to Santiago it should be less tough than that trio

Buenos Noches y Buen Camino

La Faba to Alto do Poio

Day18, Tuesday, 24th September

Chris was right. The climb to O'Cebreiro was tough but not as bad as yesterday. We stopped at Laguna de Castilla for a break. The café outside the albergue was not open but the chairs and tables are there so we can stop for a snack. Pilgrims are trickling out of the albergue across the track and disappearing into the darkness so it's time we did the same and got moving again. At last we make the last few metres up to the road where there is a vantage point to look back over the Valcarce valley. For the first time as I look down into the rising sun, I get a feeling of real elation. I climbed up that mountain, I really did. I have actually achieved something. It occurs to me that a lot of walkers were organising taxis to carry their bags to the next stop. Nothing wrong with that, it's your camino so do it the way that suits you best but I made it, bag and all, me, Terry McHugh, 64 years old and fit for nothing and I made it without any shortcuts. Hope that does not sound boastful but I do feel a real sense of achievement. Aren't those mountains beautiful?

'Going to the mountains is going home' - John Muir

We stop in O'Cebreiro for a well-earned breakfast and we see many familiar faces passing through. Franz from Sahagún is here but his group is a bit strung out so the others are not about. Mees and I had been discussing the possibility of following the road down but we missed the turn and ended up on the official Camino trail after all. Once again, I fall behind at an incline. Brierley says it's mostly downhill now. The bits that go up are not gentle slopes though so there is still some hard walking. At last there is a long fairly straight stretch going down as far as the eye can see. Mees is way off in the distance but

[133]

once again we have our arrangements made as to where we are stopping. Franz now catches up with me and walks some distance with me. Believe it or not he is carrying an umbrella. Eventually he says goodbye and moves on down the hill but two pretty girls catch his eye so he slows to walk with them and I can now catch up on him. '*Hey Franz, what do you know, I have finally passed someone*'. '*Go for it Terry,*' he replies. Of course he passed me again later and as he walked off into the distance, it was the last time I would see him.

At Alto San Roque we stop to take pictures at the *Monumento do Peregrino*. It's a bit misty up here and a cold wind is blowing so we do not dally here too long. Down past Hospital de la Condesa and we are seeing some really beautiful scenery stretched out below us; we are still 1200metres above sea level.

The map in the Brierley guide shows a gentle climb up to our days destination, Alto de Poio. Boy, does he under represent this one. The final part of the trail up to the albergue is as bad as yesterday's climb although a lot shorter. I actually am doing a whole lot worse on this climb and have made umpteen stops for water but at last I pop up over the last stretch to find myself in the courtyard of the albergue and Mees is sitting there with his café Americano and a bocadillo. He is chatting with the Dutch guy who gave me the rehydration salts back in El Acebo. As I mentioned then, he had a tee shirt the same as Mees. In the Netherlands there is a famous walk sometimes called the Nijmegen or more correctly the *4 Daagse March*. Participants get this tee shirt and a medal from the royal house of the Netherlands for completing the walk and both Mees and this other chap have both done it, in fact both have done it more than once, three times in Mees's case. By the time I finished

[134]

this book, he had added a fourth, guaranteeing him a place in the centenary walk in 2016.

This albergue is part of a café/bar. There is another hostel/hotel across the road but there is nothing else in this village. At least we won't have to go looking for dinner tonight as we can get it right here in the bar. We now have a leisurely 10km downhill walk to Triacastela tomorrow then another fairly easy walk (20km) to Sarria. Sarria to Portomarín the following day looks very tough so might take two days or maybe a stop just short of the drop down to Portomarín because it's a pretty hefty climb up to Alto Páramo and as I have said, when God made me he forgot to put in the uphill gear, but those are considerations for tomorrow.

There is nothing in this sleepy little place so nothing to do but lie on our beds until dinner time in about 4 hours. Patrick Terence turned up. I met Jolly again when she stopped for a snack and she told me about the guy back in La Faba who annoyed me so much. His name was Stefan and he has a bit of a bad reputation. Seems he invited two middle aged ladies outside to settle a disagreement. He sounds even more repugnant than before and I hope I do not meet him again. I also hope he finds what he is looking for on this camino. Jolly has a Miraculous Medal that she got in Rabe just like dozens of other peregrinos. She felt it was special so had kept it but had no idea what it was. Obviously she is not Catholic so I do my best to explain it to her and then she leaves and glances back as she shouts 'goodbye Terr'. I never seen her again, more's the pity. I really liked that young lady.

Dinner is not so good, edible but not great. Could have been worse though, some people went across the road to the hotel and the owner seemed to be, to say the least, a little eccentric and scary. It's an easy walk tomorrow so I think I will sleep a little easier tonight

Buenos Noches y Buen Camino

[135]

Alto de Poio to Triacastela

Day 19, Wednesday, 25th September

Today we took a little bit of a lie in. The distance to Triacastela is just 13km which should take us about 3 hours. However, it turned out to be harder than it looked on the map. The descent to Biduedo was a fairly pleasant walk with some beautiful scenery. We are still pretty high up in the mountains and we can look down and realise just how high we have climbed. It is

 pretty awesome and many months later as I write this, I still find it hard to believe I actually did it and have a strange urge to do it again. At the time of walking however I was finding it incredible that anyone would be daft enough to do this more than once.

Today I saw a strange sight in a café where we had stopped for breakfast. A peregrino came in with his walking staff and shell. He was dressed like he was out for a Sunday stroll with light chinos, fancy shoes and a pastel coloured jumper wrapped around his shoulders. Behind him in proper hiking gear and carrying the rucksacks were his wife and their disabled daughter. We would see him later in Triacastela marching along with his two female carriers behind him. Very strange indeed. The trail down to our day's destination, is very steep, rocky and dusty and without my walking poles, I could have come a cropper on more than one occasion.

As I have already said, we are now operating mostly from Mees's Dutch guidebook, and from the recommendations in it we pick an albergue at the end of the town rather than at the start. For an extra €7, the hospitalero does all our washing and drying and he also has free internet and printing facilities. As we are now only 155km from Santiago and, if we follow the schedule Mees has worked out, we will arrive October 3rd. It is time I took the plunge so I booked my flights home. I have chosen the Saturday flight, the dearest one but come hell or high water I will be home on October 5th. I am able to print out the booking but not the boarding card as the computer does not seem to be set up to handle the pop up screen. Of course, maybe it's me having a language problem but as long as it's booked, Aer Lingus don't charge for check in at the airport. According to Brierley, it's just 6 days to Santiago and we have allowed ourselves 8 or 9 days to do it so we should be fine. Besides, I have now come to trust Mees completely. He was a petty officer in the Dutch navy and well used to organising things so if he says we will make it, we will make it. As he often says *'Mees is always right, even when he is wrong, he is right.'* He refers to himself in the third person. You just got to love this guy.

So far, this camino has been a heck of an experience. There are so many different peregrinos with many different reasons for walking. Some have religious reasons and want to be close to God, some have problems and feel the solitude will help them sort out their heads, some just want a hiking adventure and some like me haven't a clue why they came on this trek, although I am fast discovering that it is like the 'retreats' of old that people went on to renew their faith. Then there are those who just want to be able to go home and boast about how fast they have done El Camino and believe me, they have the blisters and injuries to prove it. I wonder why some peregrinos seem to want to turn a pilgrimage into a race. I understand that not everyone is as lucky as me with no time constraints and have jobs to get back to but boasting about how far they can walk while piercing blisters on red raw feet is just beyond my comprehension.

This town of Triacastela is named after three castles that used to be here but unfortunately, there is no trace of them remaining. The centre of town is still very old and as such is very narrow, too narrow for vehicles so it is pedestrian only. A strange thing happened here. We had stopped at a bar for our afternoon snack and I spotted they had cider on tap. Now, I do enjoy a cold cider on a hot day so I just had to try it. Spanish cider is good but I had never come across it before and never seen it again unfortunately. Anyway, back to the strange event. We sat down outside the bar to enjoy our drinks and as usual, we were served with some complimentary tapas. Today the snack was a large bowl of peanuts served in a double bowl, the second bowl for the shells. We had just about finished when some more peregrinos sat at a table facing us with the same fare on their table. Nothing strange about all this you might say and you would be right but suddenly, without warning we heard the sound of a strong wind hurtling down the narrow street. It seemed to come from nowhere and in an instant, a warm sunny afternoon changed to a veritable gale turning over tables and blowing peanuts everywhere. As quick as it had risen, it disappeared and it was a warm sunny afternoon again. Just one gust and that was it. I have never experienced anything like it before or since. The bar owner never took it under his notice, he just lifted up his tables replaced the peanuts and went about his business as if nothing had happened. Maybe it was a sign of the weather to come but for now apart from a light shower, it is fine.

Once again, I have no recollection of dinner tonight but it must have been good as I recorded it in my daily journal and I also commented that the wine was not great.

Everything is going to plan now but it's not my plan. All along this journey I have made decisions that at the time were not significant or in the case of taking a train or bus, forced on me as I was falling behind schedule. However, there have been unforeseen consequences to each decision I have taken. Like the day I met the Blessed Virgin and Mees in the same town. Had I not decided to walk on that day I would not have come across the apparition site and I would not have met my friend and travelling companion, Mees. Would I be here today without him? Probably not. Was it Mary calling me to the town named after her so that I could discover her amazing story and find the companion I needed to get me through the difficult days in the mountains? I believe so. Yes, I do believe that Jesus and Mary are guiding me through my Guardian Angel. I had come to believe that this angel was just a story we told children, like a fairy godmother, but now I have found a trust in him that I have not known since I was a child. I am not a religious person but I certainly am finding more reasons to have faith these last few weeks. I am praying more or rather I am having a conversation with someone I am developing a friendly relationship with. Just as I am learning to trust my friend Mees, I am growing to believe more in Jesus as a real entity in my life that I can trust to look after and help me and send along the people I need to ease my problems on this Camino. I know now that I will complete it with God's help and I will attend Mass and receive communion in Santiago. I also know that no matter what happens in my life from this day on, a little part of me will remain here in Spain and my soul will be lighter because the doubts about my faith are slowly but surely fading. But that's enough for today. All that's left is to decide which route to take tomorrow. Follow the Camino route as described by Brierley or take the option to the monastery at Samos like my son did last year. We decide to stick to the main Camino as it would add far too much time to our journey, so decision made it's off to bed

Buenos Noches y Buen Camino

Triacastela to Sarria

Day 20, Thursday, 26th September

There is a little café open just down the Calle from the albergue so today we walk with a good breakfast inside us. It is just past 7am when we finally set out. I am so glad I met Mees as he is a great companion, a friend I will remember for life.

It is a tough slog up to Alto Riocabo as it rises approximately 300m but as it's the start of the day, I am fresh enough to make it without too much trouble and can boastfully say that I have done tougher. We pass through a village called San Xil but I have no idea how to pronounce that. Just before we entered the town, we passed a rest area with a fuenta with a large shell motif. I realise now that the biggest problem about walking in September is that the mornings get darker each day as we  head towards the autumn and eventually Winter. It is too dark to get a good photo of this fountain and until it gets light, there may as well be no scenery at all as I can't see a thing that is not within range of my head torch. Fortunately, the photo I did take was good enough to be suitable for electronic enhancement.

By the time we have reached the top, my backpack has all but broken my back. It just does not sit right and constantly falls to the left so that even though it is early in the day, my left shoulder is aching. A short stop for a rest and a snack eases the pain and it's all downhill now to Sarria.

John Brierley describes the trail as *'pleasant forest paths'*. In Ireland we would call them bloody Bohreens. Yes they are tree lined but that's as close as it gets to the description in the guide book. They are better described as rough tough cattle trails, rocky, dusty and treacherous. At least though, the trees keep the sun off us and it is just as well as it's getting hotter by the minute.

Out in the open, I start to struggle not with the terrain which is quite good, but with the heat. The sun would pick today to

[140]

come out as I started with less water than usual and for the first time I have emptied my bottles, approximately 2L. I usually carry 2.5L. But we are in Sarria, not all the way in, but inside the city boundary, only just. We have chosen to stop at the first albergue, A Pedra, right beside the tourist office. I check in with them to get their sello and find they are pushing the rumour that has been circulating amongst the peregrinos for the last few days. They are telling everyone that from here to Santiago, they must get two sellos per day. What I come to call, the walking sello and the sleeping sello. Now this is true for pilgrims starting from Sarria but for those who have come from further afield, only one sello a day is needed. Don't let anyone tell you any different. I know I am right because it says so in my credentials provided by the Irish Confraternity. But it does not matter. If they were to refuse me a Compostela well who cares. I know how far I have walked, God knows as does my family and my good friend Mees. Jumping prematurely to the end of my story, I was right, just one stamp per day.

This albergue has been a good choice. There is a Correos just round the corner so I am determined to get the weight of the backpack down by posting a couple of kilograms to myself in Santiago. I actually got 2.9kilo into the box, 2.9 less on my back. If it should get lost the only thing I would cry about would be my Rohan shorts.

When I get back from the Correos, we go on a little shopping trip and I am tempted by an advertisement for ice cream. I can't resist it, I just must have it and to hell with my diabetes. It was delicious especially on such a hot day. As I enjoy it, two American pilgrims ask if I know the way to the hotel, Alfonso IX. This is described in the guide as a luxury establishment. How nice it must be to have the wealth to be able to stay in luxury hotels instead of albergues. I am feeling a bit jealous but not jealous enough to not help them. Besides, it is easy, they are standing right outside it. They, as we say in Ireland, could not see the wood for the trees. I hope they had a good night but I will bet it was not as good as ours.

Dinner is served in the bar next door and it is some meal. Soup, salad, tortilla and eggplant pasties. I don't know what they are called in Spanish but in every language they are called delicious. When the meal was finished there was still a bottle of wine left and some cheese. Well, as I had become known as the Irish guy who never leaves any wine behind, I just had to finish it. Not all on my own mind you but I reckon I had more than

[141]

half. The hospitalero then brought out an after dinner liqueur. I forget the name of it but if I could remember it, I would be scouring the off licences at home until I found a bottle. As we all enjoyed it so much he decided that we must try his home made stuff. I don't know if this stuff is legal but who cares, it was fantastic. He had made it from acorns of which there is an abundance around Sarria, in places they lay on the ground as thick as a carpet. I will sleep well tonight with all this lovely food and drink inside me

Buenos Noches y Buen Camino

Sarria to Mercadoiro

Day 21, Friday, 27th September

Well this is it. The final stage on El Camino de Santiago. This is the minimum starting place to walk from if you want to receive a Compostela. That is the certificate issued by the Cathedral authorities to confirm the pilgrim has completed the minimum requirement. For fairly fit people starting from here, it should take just a week. Many Spanish start from here as a Compostela is a good thing to have on your CV and I believe it entitles the bearer to discount travel home from Santiago. For the few peregrinos who stick to the old tradition of retracing their steps, it can be used to get accommodation in the albergues on the way back. In medieval times there were no trains, buses or planes so the pilgrim had only one way of getting home, walk.

Unfortunately, the Camino becomes a bit of a race from this point. It's not so bad in late September when the numbers walking have started to decrease but at the height of the summer, there are so many walkers that albergues fill up quickly so if you want a bed, you have to race. People pass by in their best clothes some carrying a pole and a shell, others with umbrellas but few with backpacks any bigger than those my kids went to school with. They are cheerful and friendly and greet you with the usual *'Buen Camino'*. Sometimes, in a very un-Christian way, when I am tired and the pack is digging into my shoulders, I think to myself, *'Touregrinos!!!, easy for them to say'*. I always regret it afterwards when I remember that the Camino is a very personal thing between the pilgrim and God and everyone has the right to do it in their own way. However there are some who really annoy the long distance walker. The ones who walk for a couple of hours having sent their luggage ahead by taxi and when they get a stamp on their credentials around lunch time, get a taxi to take them to the days destination. They then get another stamp to meet the requirement of two stamps per day if you only walk from Sarria. By using this trick, they get to Santiago by only walking around half of the final 100km.

Today we started early but when we found a café open for breakfast, we sat a little longer than usual. As we left Sarria, we were overtaken by a pilgrim in a pinstripe suit, white trainers and a small suitcase tied to his back. On the suitcase is one word, *'Ireland'*. The guy is twirling a long staff quite professionally and I remark to Mees that had his suitcase said Northern Ireland, I would have sworn he was an Orangeman from Belfast the way he twirled that pole. When I met my Swedish friends later they told me that he was a fireman from Dublin who had lost a wager and was walking for charity. I hope he collected plenty of Euros for it.

Dark clouds are now gathering above us and eventually, the skies opened and it started to bucket down. Mees has a poncho and I have a waterproof jacket. Today I will find the difference between the two and regret my decision to leave my poncho at home.

It is all uphill now and Mees starts to pull away but as he has the only light blue poncho among all the other pilgrims, I can keep him in sight. We have agreed to stop short of Portomarín in a place called Mercadoiro. I had actually been looking forward to arriving in the square in Portomarín having seen it on the webcams that broadcast from there but later I will see the wisdom of stopping short.

By the time I reached the town of Morgade which is just over the first peak of today's walk, I have lost sight of Mees and the water is dripping out of me. I may be dry under my jacket but my trousers are soaking and clinging to me and just altogether uncomfortable. For the first time I feel that Jesus is not walking with me and doubts are creeping in just as they did back in Castrojeriz on Good Friday when I turned back and went home. But of course he is still with me, but I reckon Jesus wears a poncho. I finally find a little bar and adjoining barn where all my friends are crammed in and they smile when they see me arrive with the water dripping out of me. They are all enjoying a coffee and talking about the next stage of today's walk. They say the Lord works in mysterious ways. Well it's a mystery to me how he got all these people to wait long enough until a rather despondent Irishman arrived. I just don't like the rain; we get more than our fair share in auld Erin. Then I spotted the blue poncho and the blue rucksack at the back of the barn, Mees is here. I dump my own gear and go into the bar and there he is with his usual Café Americano. A couple of pilgrims are touting around looking for someone to share a taxi with them to Portomarín and I have to say, I was not a little tempted, I was tempted a lot. One guy who has injured his leg takes them up on their offer but we decline. Just then I hear another Irish voice and I take the opportunity to have a chat. When it is time to push on into the rain again, he says

[144]

something only an Irishman could say. *"Sure back home, this is what we would call a 'soft day'"*. A typical country man with a typical country phrase. But it worked, it sent me off laughing.

The camino now follows the road through Ferrerios to Cruce Momientos. If I may, I will quote John Brierley when he says in his guide,

'*This is rural Galicia at her best; wet and green with the sweet smell and squelch of liquid cow dung underfoot*'.

Doesn't that sound lovely? I wonder John if you ever walked it in a continuous downpour that didn't let up for a moment. It was certainly wet, it could have been any colour through the rain and the cow dung, it did not smell so sweet at all. Maybe someday I will come back and hopefully get better weather to enjoy this section but for now it is just a description in Mr Brierley's book. I know I may at times sound a little critical of John Brierley but really, his book is more than worth the purchase price although if I ever come back, it will be his smaller lighter map booklet I will be carrying. It is just a case of at times you need someone to complain about and Mr Brierley can't answer back, sorry John.

After a steep climb up to Alto Páramo we drop down to Momientos were we leave the road and take to the trails. Well, I say trails and normally they probably are just that, but today they are fast flowing streams. Oh let's call a spade a spade, they are raging torrents. Initially I tried to pick my way between dry spots sticking up out of the water but as they became less and less I gave up and just ploughed on into it. This is so bad that if there were anyone called Noah about, he would be getting out his hammer and nails. Mees has disappeared into the distance again but I am not worried, there would not have been much opportunity for conversation today anyway.

I remember many years ago, a comedian, Dave Allen, who was a bit irreverent. He used to say that God must have a sense of humour otherwise he would have struck him down long ago. Today I know he has a sense of humour. I am tired, wet and hungry and once again getting a bit depressed. The only upside is that my boots are waterproof so my feet are fairly dry for now. Nothing I can do about water running down my legs and into my socks though. But back to the Lord's sense of humour. What should he send me but a singing Italian. Really, he is

[145]

singing his heart out in this rain as he comes up behind me. As he passes me I notice he is covered from head to toe in mud. He sees me looking at him and simply laughs and says *'I fall'* and off he goes leaving me laughing. But it gets better. As I come round the next bend there is a broken drain pipe on a farm building and the water is pouring from it. You guessed it. The singing Italian makes a beeline for it and stands underneath washing off the mud. In his broken English he says if he must be wet, at least he can be clean. His friends and I and a couple of others stop to watch and someone breaks into a rendition of Gene Kelly's *'Singing in the Rain'* and then everyone joins in and we stand there in the bucketing rain singing like a load of fools. God has a way of raising my spirits on this walk. I am convinced more than ever that he is with me and wants me to finish this. Every time I am feeling down or having doubts about my ability to continue, he sends something or someone to help me. Too many things have gone right when I at times thought I was making the wrong decision for it to be just a coincidence. Don't be fooled here, I have never been particularly religious. I am what you might call 'a Sunday Catholic', have I said that before, who has had more doubts about his faith than he cares to have. I envy the people who have a simple faith and just believe without question. But the more I walk, with my solitary thoughts, the more I find myself believing and conversing with Jesus, Mary and my Guardian Angel. At this rate I will be holding prayer meetings soon, better take it easy with all these strange thoughts.

Still the rain comes down. I know they say it can rain in Galicia but this is ridiculous. How much further do I have to go? How many more kilometres? As I round a bend I see a Guinness sign hanging from a wall and standing underneath it is Mees. Welcome to Mercadoiro. I thought I still had a way to go but here we are at the end of our days walk. This village has an official population of one but tonight it will be at least three as Mees and I are going no further. Its 5km more to Portomarín but I am glad we are not walking on in this rain. I think God has a way of preventing the Pilgrim from getting too proud of himself as he nears Santiago because, you know, it is hard to feel proud when the water is dripping out of you.

I am soaked to the skin. The water has got into my wallet and my credentials are soaked. The ink from some of the sellos is running and smearing the pages. In my other pockets, the receipt for the stuff I sent to Santiago is sodden as is my flight booking and my Brierley guide, it will take days to dry out.

[146]

Fortunately, I had put my diary in a plastic bag so it's OK. So is my passport and money. The floor of the albergue is soaking as the water runs out of our clothes, onto a bench then onto the floor. There is no way to dry anything other than hang it on a clothes airer in the front entrance. The rain did eventually get into my boots but fortunately, I have a spare pair of foot beds that I bought way back in Castrojeriz. Not great but dry and they will do until I get the good ones dried.

There is a garden between the albergue and the bar/restaurant. The rain has stopped for a while and the flies have come out. These damned things are everywhere. It occurs to me that I have never seen a spider anywhere along this way. They need to import some to keep the flies down.

As we sit in the bar enjoying a beer, it starts to rain again. An American couple, the ones we met in Mazariffe and have met on and off along the way come in and the four of us just sit and watch the rain fall. Not a bad afternoon really. Seriously, I am not joking, we really enjoyed it. Good company, good beer and the rain was out there and we weren't.

Dinner that night was excellent. Maybe after today's rain, anything would seem good but I really enjoyed it.

It's time for bed but before I go to sleep, I say my night prayers as usual but throw in an extra one for better weather tomorrow. Is he listening? Of course he is as I will find out in the morning

Buenos Noches y Buen Camino

Mercadoiro to Ligonde

Day 22, Saturday, 28th September

I had hoped that the restaurant of the albergue would be open this morning but no joy. It's really dark this morning and a bit chilly. The walk down to Portomarín is a bit hard to follow in the dark and the only other pilgrim on the road is following our lights. After a couple of almost wrong turns we make it down to the road and it's a straight walk to town. Hopefully we can get some breakfast here. As we cross the long bridge into the town we can see streams of peregrinos heading out. The entrance to this town is the one I have seen in photos, a large staircase that we must climb, ouch. At the top we find a restaurant/albergue but no food, just coffee. We have a bit of bread in our bag so that will have to do. Well back on the trail again and still hungry.

It's a tough climb up out of the river valley to Monte San Antonio. It is raining on and off but nothing too heavy. From here it's a fairly gentle incline that parallels the main road and criss crosses it a few times. Along the way I spot a familiar face, the Irish/Canadian lady, Siobhan, whom I met way back in Castrojeriz and she remembers me. Was that really 19 days ago? I can't believe that I have walked for that long. I remember before I retired, I always found some excuse for not going for a walk at lunchtime and that was just a flat walk along the shore but the tiny little hill back up to the university was more than I could handle. Here I am now having walked non-stop for 19 days down valleys and up mountains covering 400km. The old phrase my Mum used when we were misbehaving as kids, *'God give me strength'* is really not just an empty phrase. He really does give you strength, not just spiritual but physical. The strength to carry on putting one foot in front of the other when your body is screaming, enough is enough.

At last we arrive in a little town called Gonzar where we can finally get something to eat. Every pilgrim on the Camino seems to be here. Mees is already there as I had slowed down to walk and talk with a lady limping along on walking sticks. She is crippled with arthritis and yet has made it all the way from St Jean Pied de Port, a truly amazing achievement and I am complaining about a few hills. It is about 11am so it's more of a brunch than a breakfast. This is the first place I have been to in Spain that expects to be paid when you place your order.

Everyone else has waited until we were finished eating and ready to leave.

It's a steep climb up out of Gonzar through Hospital to Sierra Ligonde. Mees has gone ahead but is never out of sight for long. It was along this stretch that I heard something that kept us laughing for some time. Two American ladies came by pretty quickly. In a long American drawl, one proclaims that she really misses her Merrells (a brand of walking shoe). As we come around a bend there is a bus parked outside a better class of restaurant than the one we just left. Oh, there is the bus proclaims the other; you can get your Merrells now. Touregrinos!! What would you do with them I laugh?

As I walked out of Hospital I once again hear a familiar voice. Its Grumpy again. He is down to just two cigarettes a day he tells me. A bit of a cool breeze has come up and he is feeling the cold so stops to put on something warm. Up ahead his father has stopped to wait for him. No stamina in youngsters today I remark as I pass his dad and he agrees with me. Of course they pass me not long after; everyone does. As they enter the little village of Ventas de Narón they take a branch to the right while I keep left. There is a café on both branches and they are stopping for coffee. I never saw them again. I had hoped I would meet them in Santiago but it was not to be. At the next café, as I approach, I see Mees leaving so I decide to walk on and forego my café con leche for today.

I have now passed the peak and am on the descent to Ligonde. Mees and I had discussed stopping here but it was not definite. If he is waiting for me, we are stopping; if not then it's the next town. As I come up on the outskirts there he is waiting for me and there goes Siobhan heading down the hill. I will never see her again either. The weather is not looking good. It's been trying hard to rain for a while now and after yesterday's soaking I ask Jesus if he can keep the rain off long enough for us to get indoors. I know that to some, this may sound daft but I asked in all sincerity.

This is an ancient hamlet and we are looking for a restored municipal albergue called Escuela. What we find is an equally ancient albergue, Fuente del Peregrino run by a religious group and it is donativo. We decide to stop here as we think we have missed the municipal one. A young girl is sitting outside and tells us that they will be admitting peregrinos in about 10 minutes so we wait with her. She is from Bavaria and her name is Paula.

As we sign in the hospitalero tells us that dinner is supplied but before that there is a prayer time that they would like us to attend and then there will be a movie and popcorn. This is unbelievable; all this for donation only. The hospitalero and his assistant carry our bags up to the dorm and place them on the bed for us. It's a bit tight up here. Barely enough room to make

 your way between the rows of beds and the beds in each row tight together, but it's dry and warm. Remember I said I asked God to keep the rain of till we got indoors? Well now, the skies opened and it rained continually for the rest of the night.

The prayer time at 5pm was a very emotional experience. Two Irish women and a German girl, Almut, who has lived most of her life in Mexico, have joined us. The Irish women are both teachers and are sisters. They press the hospitalero to find out which religion they are but he refuses to answer stating that we are all the children of God in this albergue. He has asked us to read little post-it notes that have been left by yesterday's pilgrims and the idea is that we will pray for them and then leave our own little notes for tomorrows pilgrims who will in their turn, pray for us. As I read the one given to me, I start to cry. I won't say here what was written as it is a private thing, suffice to say that it was a sad one. We now play a game with a deck of cards, not playing cards but pictures. The idea is that we pick a picture that best reflects our reason for being on the Camino. I choose a happy one for I have come to realise more than ever that I have had a good life. The only dark spot in our lives has been the death of our son. It does not get much darker than that but we have learned to live with the memory. We will never get over it though. The hospitalero tells us that his wife is pregnant after many years of marriage. They thought they would never have a child so they have adopted twice. He tells me that seeing me cry when I read the note made him cry too and it meant so much to him that someone had been so touched by what he was trying to do. I never noticed him cry though. Mees now opens up and reveals his innermost thoughts. They are his and not for me to write down. It's enough to say that he has had a sad few years and is looking

[150]

for some peace of mind on his Camino. He tells me later that he had no intention when he set out of ever sharing these thoughts with anyone. I think he is glad we stopped here. Almut and Paula also share their innermost thoughts although I think the Irish women held back somewhat. I got the feeling that they were uncomfortable with the whole thing and suspicious when the hospitalero would not declare which religion he was. He was South American; his boss who seemed to be taking a less prominent roll other than playing the guitar and singing, was Spanish. I assume they were Catholic but it does not really matter. Someone later told us that they thought they were Jehovah Witnesses but there was no attempt to do any conversions and no preaching of the Bible so I doubt it. They were just a group living the Christian way. On facebook, they are Fuente de Peregrino.

The movie is a budget version of the life of Jesus and, true to their word, they supplied popcorn. That was the only thing that did not seem right, eating popcorn while watching the Passion. A little mouse that I had seen earlier creeping out of a hole in the old stone wall comes to join us and causes a bit of a commotion with the girls. The hospitalero tells us he has been meaning to do something about it all summer but just can't bring himself to kill it. For some reason the Irish women have not joined us for the movie. I think they were afraid it may have been some sort of propaganda but they missed a good evening. I hope they kept the copy that each peregrino was given.

Another great dinner with lots of wine. I had thought, as it was a religious albergue, there would be no alcohol but after dessert and coffee there were liqueurs. I had a brandy. And these guys are asking for nothing, just a donation.

Normally I finish my journal at this point but tonight is different. In the middle of the night Almut woke Mees and asked him to stop snoring. It's not me, he says, it is him and he points to me as I have just awakened. As a few others are now awake they all have a good laugh. Not sure who they were laughing at, Almut or me but apparently I went back to sleep and did not snore again the rest of the night

Buenos noches y Buen Camino

[151]

Ligonde to Melide

Day23, Sunday, 29th September

Although we are up early we are not starting early. The hospitaleros have left breakfast out for us and last night had asked that the first person down should switch on the coffee machine and kettle. That job falls to me. There is cereal, bread for toasting, jam and cartons of various juices. This is one good breakfast with really good company. The cornflakes are LIDL brand and must have been good as Paula has three bowls. She will be well filled up for the trek ahead.

We left the albergue about 7:40 after cleaning up the dining area and leaving a good donation. A night like that would normally have cost me up to €20 euro for bed and a dinner not as good as we got here. As we set of up the road in the pitch dark, we find the albergue we meant to stop in last night. We hadn't passed it after all but I believe we were not meant to stop there; Jesus wanted us to stop where we did so that we could come to know ourselves, our friends and him much better. Once again, I believe I have been guided by a higher power. A small insignificant decision that turned out to have a huge meaning for me and my friend for life, Mees.

It's an uneventful walk today, all tarmac, or as an American called it, black top, to Palas de Rei. The only thing of note was the peregrino who passed us on a uni-cycle. The rain has started again. Not as heavy as last night, more of an Irish style drizzle. I am conscious of the fact that it is Sunday morning and I am hoping I may come across a church where I can get to misa. It's a bit of a problem on the Camino. Because of the time we have to start out in the mornings, it is too early for mass and by the time most churches are celebrating the Eucharist, we are deep in the countryside or on top of a mountain. To steal a few words from John Brierley when he described La Cruz de Ferro a million miles ago,

> "a grander chapel surrounds us that will remain forever open and welcoming".

Thanks for those words Mr Brierley, they convey just how I feel as I take in the beauty of this world that God has given us, even with this 'soft day' as we say in Ireland. That quote from John Brierley reminds me of another from John Muir, an early 20th century author and conservationist.

"I'd rather be in the mountains thinking of God, than in a church thinking about the mountains"

As we arrive in Palas de Rei, I spot a church that is open and looks like it is ready for mass. Unfortunately, I have just missed it but at least I can stop and pray and thank God for getting me this far and sending so many good people to make this an experience of a lifetime that I will never forget.

The caretaker is in the sacristy and he invites us in to get a sello. There is a basket for donations but I have left all my euro coins back in Ligonde so I drop a couple of pounds sterling into it. I hope he didn't mind when he counted it later.

It has been my experience that on a Sunday in Spain, everything closes but today is the exception. A sports shop is not for missing out on the passing pilgrim trade, so I pop in and buy a cheap poncho. There is no doubt, the poncho is more effective than the rain jacket and as it is starting to rain again, I think it is a worthwhile purchase. We continued our 16.5km hike through to O' Coto where we planned to stop for lunch. The poncho is proving its worth as it is raining again, not as heavy as when we hiked to Mercadoiro the other day but heavy enough. After lunch we set out again for Melide at just after noon thinking we would make our destination about 3pm. We are extending the length of time we are walking each day now that Santiago is almost close enough to taste. As it is now mostly downhill, we made better time than we thought and arrived at about 14:15. Just to finish the day off badly, Melide is on the other side of a river valley so there is a short sharp incline up to the town which in the blazing heat, now that the sun has come out, is tough going. As usual, Mees has walked on a bit faster but I can see him waiting for me at the top of the hill. The Brierley guide says there are two albergues in Melide but there are in fact four. The first one is off to the right of the Camino across some open ground very visible from the road. Upstairs it is a hostel and downstairs it is an albergue. Just inside the door there is a bar/restaurant. Just by way of keeping the record straight, this albergue is called Elide and the other one not mentioned is Pierro.

I am really struggling as I enter the albergue. Getting rid of a lot of weight from my backpack does not seem to have helped much as it still feels a ton weight and is dragging the shoulders out of me. I wonder if I am strapping it up properly. We are greeted by a young girl, no more than 19 or 20 I would guess, and she recognises that I am struggling and offers to take my bag for me. I am not that far gone yet, besides Mees would never let me live it down. She offers to do our laundry for us, how nice is that? After we have showered and changed the thirst is upon us so we order a couple of beers from the bar and go out to sit in the patio. It's a nice change from this morning's rain. As we enjoy our beer, the girl comes out and asks if she can take our photo. Of course we agree, two old men being photographed by a pretty young señorita, how flattered are we? A few minutes later she comes back with a bowl of mixed nuts and fruit. I love the way Spanish bars offer free snacks with the beer and, even better, she then returns with two small slices of pizza. This is what I call being treated royally.

It's now time to rest. Mees loves to have a lie down in the afternoon and listen to his music, fairly classical stuff. I don't like to disturb this private time he takes each day so I make myself scarce.

The batteries in my camera are done; the shortest time I have ever got from a Duracell set but then the camera is acting up. Somewhere around Foncebaden it got damp into it, not rain, condensation and I think it may also have taken a knock. Anyway, it has taken to switching itself on and starting to beep. Not what I want in the middle of the night. There are times that I have taken it out to find it is switched on in playback mode so that is probably eating the batteries. The girl points me in the direction of a filling station where I get new ones. Everywhere else is closed for Sunday. Now, this is the Spanish Sunday I am used to.

The new batteries seem to have fixed the camera and it is working as it should do now. I should not need any more this trip. It's only about 53km to Santiago now and compared to the 500km I had to do from Burgos, I feel like I have really achieved something. Is it wrong to say I am slightly proud of myself? Maybe, but I am, so there. The only thing to dampen my enthusiasm today is a new blister on my left heel again. Having done 14km today in damp insoles did not help especially when I discover that the repair I had made to the damaged one with fabric plasters had come off. That is easily fixed, the blister not so easily. The usual treatment of a needle through the blister and leave the thread in helps.

Not sure what to do about dinner. The restaurant is not operating at this time of year and as this is the second last day of September a lot of albergues are closing for the year. We heard a rumour that the municipal one is already closed. I can't confirm this but, it is a fact that the Camino season is coming to an end. We are the last batch still on the trail, that is, those ahead and those a couple of days behind us. After that, the numbers will be thinning out considerably.

However, back to dinner. Surely the restaurants don't all close so we ask the girl for her advice and she tells us that there are a few places up the road and a good Pulperia. I have no clue as to what a Pulperia is but I soon find out, it is an Octopus House and I don't mean an aquarium. It seems odd to me that somewhere so far from the sea should be so fond of octopus. Anyway, we pass some restaurants in favour of the pulperia and discover they have a pilgrim menu. Once we ask for it, the wine glasses are taken away and I have a bad feeling there is no wine. Not a chance. There is no way the Spanish are ever going to offer a meal that does not include wine. The reason the glasses were taken away is so they can be replaced with earthenware drinking bowls, like simple little chalices; it's all about tradition, pilgrims do not drink from fancy wine glasses. I like this. It must be said, the wine was of a very good quality. It's the first time I have ever seen wine on tap. As you empty your bottle and want another, the waiter takes the bottle and offers it up to an optic type tap and refills it. As we get down to desert, Paula and Almut join us. Almut decides she will try the octopus. Enjoyable as she finds it, the typically over filled Spanish plate is too much for her so she asks us to share it with her. I always like to try new things, like the day, to my wife's disgust, I tried Escargot. Well I have to report that octopus is not too bad, a bit saltier than I care for, but texture and taste quite good.

A discussion broke out between the two girls with some input from Mees. Paula says she is Bavarian but Almut says she can't be as she does not speak Bavarian. She says you must be able to speak the language before claiming the nationality. I counter with the argument that I can't speak Irish but God help anyone who dares to say I am not Irish. Anyway, we leave them to it and head back to the albergue and bed

Buenos Noches y Buen Camino

[155]

Melide to Arzúa

Day 24, Monday, 30th September

I have been up since 6am but Mees lay on till nearly 7. It was almost 8:05 before we got walking having stopped for breakfast but we are not going so far today so the late start is not a problem. The Brierley guide has warned us that even though the profile map does not really show it, there are a lot of little river valleys which means for every drop down to a river there is an equally steep climb back up out of the valley. It is fairly much woodland which later in the day may have been pleasant but now on the last day of September it is still dark until well after 8 so there is not much to see as we must spend most of our time watching the conditions under foot. Given the terrain and the darkness, we made good time covering 4k in one hour. Somewhere around Boente we stopped at Das Café Deutche. This café is not mentioned in the Brierley guide but we found it in the Dutch guide that has been put together from pilgrim reports being sent back to the Dutch Association. We have found that on more than one occasion, this guide has been the best and if there were an English version, I think it would be a top seller.

At the café, we met Paula again, quietly writing up her journal so we joined her for a coffee. This was to be the last time we were to meet this young pilgrim and I hope she did really well in the exams she was so worried about. The two Irish sisters also arrived and stopped for a chat as did the Swedish couple. I do regret not getting their names and contacts as they were very friendly people. The lady for some reason greeted me with a hug and said they were so glad to see me. I first met them on the road from Carrion and today, this moment in this café would be the last time we would meet. I remember as she walked behind me for a while she was singing 'Somewhere Over the Rainbow' and only now that I am home do I see a connection. Follow the yellow brick road; follow the yellow arrows. I wonder did she see the connection too. Hope they found what they were looking for on this Camino.

Along the road there are strange little buildings raised on plinths. They are called Horreos and are a feature of Galicia. The purpose of them is to store corn and the plinths keep them up away from dampness and vermin. To the best of my knowledge, there is nothing like them anywhere else in the world.

We arrived in Arzúa around noon and got checked in to an albergue in the main street that had its own restaurant and extensive rooftop laundry; a nice clean and comfortable place. It has been a good day and it is just as well we stopped at noon. It is getting really hot now. Has the wet weather gone for good so that we can walk into Santiago dry? I hope so.

After the customary shower and change of clothes it is time for the afternoon beer. It is getting to be a bit of a habit now. As we lounge outside a pavement bar watching the peregrinos go by, who should come hobbling up the hill but Almut. Wonder should it be Almud, I never thought to ask how to spell her name. Hope she does not mind. She is suffering from tendonitis and is full of praise for the people who have helped her get this far. Some guy, I think she said he was Australian, even carried her backpack for her for a good part of the way. If ever you want to experience Christian kindness at first hand, then walk the Camino; it has to be the most unique pilgrimage anywhere in the world. Most others are by plane to a shrine or city and then home the same way but this must be the only one that involves a long distance hike, putting up with many hardships along the way. And it is just these hardships that bring out the best in people. Jesus is at work at every kilometre along the way urging pilgrims on and moving them to proclaim his ways not in theory but in practice. If all the world's leaders had to walk the camino before being allowed to take up office this would be a much better world. It just amazes me that this could be in a country that from the mid-30s through the 50s could be the last bastion of mass state killings in Europe. Maybe it is no wonder that the Camino was almost extinct during the dictatorship of Franco. Christianity was on the defensive in those dark days but James was called upon once again to re-establish his camino and bring pilgrims in their hundreds of thousands back to the Way.

We have decided to get some washing done as there is a huge bank of washers and driers on the rooftop terrace. Each machine has a number and there is a corresponding numbered slot machine. Someone must have got their wires crossed as nothing seems to work as it should. Does not matter which slot you put your money in, it just adds time onto machine number one but by the time we figure this out there are hours on it rather than minutes so we just have to queue up for our turn. There is a lady doing ironing for some folk but my clothes are all non-iron so I do not need to avail of her services.

I have lifted the last of my money so have €240 in my pocket. That should be plenty. The days are really starting to slip away now, just two more Brierley days to go. I hope he does not mind me using his name like this but it's just what we called them. Of course, we won't do the Brierley days, we have planned for three, 19km to O Pedrouzo tomorrow, 15.5km the next day to San Marcos/Monte del Gozo and then it's a short 4.7km walk into Santiago in time for the pilgrim mass at noon. Mees is really looking forward to the mass more than I am which is strange as he is not Catholic but is one of the most Christian people I have ever met. Monte del Gozo by the way means mount of joy. The joy the pilgrims of old would experience as they could see the lights of Santiago below them after their long hikes. For them it was a walk from their own front door somewhere in Europe. There were no plane journeys to Biarritz and train to St Jean for them. That was a real pilgrimage.

The restaurant was first class. I really enjoyed my meal and I got home made chips almost as good as Margaret makes. The lady at the next table could not finish her bottle of wine and asked if we would like it. As I said before, I don't leave good wine behind so Mees and I polished it off

Buenos Noches y Buen Camino

Arzua to O Pedrouzo

Day 25, Tuesday 1st October

On paper, today seemed pretty easy but it started out wet, hot and humid so it took a while to get into our stride. There is something wrong with Mees as he is keeping up with me rather than the other way round and when we stop for coffee somewhere around A Calzada if I remember correctly (I forgot to write it down), Mees tells me he is suffering from stomach cramps but after a good coffee and a bite to eat he is fine again. A female pilgrim approaches me and asks if I am from 'northern' Ireland but I say I am from Ireland. She says she is from Derry but seems a little miffed that I won't say 'northern' Ireland. It is a strange one. She says Derry, not Londonderry yet is annoyed because I won't say 'northern' Ireland. We settle for saying I am from the north. Don't know what to make of that but I never seen her again.

My left foot is acting up again and it is becoming difficult to walk any distance at any kind of speed but I must push myself on to our daily destination. I ask Mees if he would mind stopping again for another coffee as we reach Santa Irene, not

that I needed it, I just wanted to rest my foot. Well rested we make the last push into Arca (O Pedrouzo) another one of those Spanish towns with two names; I thought we had left that behind in the Basque country but it seems not. We know we are getting close as there are now road signs pointing to Santiago.

So here we are in Arca. The last stage is all that's left. Barring a tragedy there is nothing to stop us. Talking about tragedies, Celtic lost in their latest European game tonight; just can't stay away from the football. Tomorrow we do 16km to Monte del Gozo and then next day less than 5 into Santiago. I am trying hard to stop referring to distances in miles as all the road signs are in kilometres. I forget that the insular British island is the only place in Europe not to adopt the kilometre as the unit of measurement.

Today I took a top bunk for a change and I lie there thinking about the next two days. Mees and I will part and I wonder if we will ever meet again. We have resolved to keep in touch via e-mail and facebook but will I ever see him again. He has become a very close friend who has been more than a little responsible for getting me to this point. I will miss him greatly when we go our separate ways. I have become used to his smiling face every day and his constant reminder that *'Mees is always right, even when he is wrong he is right'*. You don't realise it my friend but you have been a guardian angel to me and meeting you has been very much a part of God's plan for me. Thanks for everything my friend, I will never forget you

Buenos Noches y Buen Camino

Arca to Monte del Gozo

Day 26, Wednesday, 2nd October

Today we stayed in bed until the sun came up. There is no point walking in the dark anymore. We will have to do it on our last morning so may as well have one day walking in the sunshine from the start.

We had a good breakfast and for the first time, we were last out of the albergue. There is no need to rush anymore as we can almost taste and smell our goal now and today we will enter the region of Santiago.

At first it was a good walk; no rain, slightly overcast, not too warm, perfect weather for walking. There were a couple of hills to climb but knowing they were the last made them seem smaller and I negotiated them with little or no difficulty. Maybe at this late stage, my fitness is finally kicking in; a bit late I have to say. However as we passed the airport at Labacolla, my foot started to hurt again. Just my luck, I also think I have developed a blister. I have been very lucky regarding blisters, only had a few and because I treated them immediately, they never became a problem. In fact, using the foot balm specially made for pilgrims to reduce friction has been a great boon. It is like Vaseline and if anyone had told me back home that I should put Vaseline on my feet before walking, I would have thought they were mad but believe me, it really works.

At last we stopped at a café for a much needed rest. They have hamburgers, wow. I can't resist it so I order one along with my coffee. The lady behind the counter must have taken a shine to me because before she gave me my coffee she used a straw to draw a happy face in the froth. No one else got that and boy, were they jealous.

My foot is well rested so off we go on the climb to Monte del Gozo. It's all road walking now, up past the local TV station and on past a caravan holiday park. There is a vineyard here but unlike others along the way, this one has wire around the boundary to stop pilgrims picking grapes, but me being me, I just gotta do it. I poke my fingers through the wire and pluck two. They were lovely. As we come round a bend Mees laughs and points at the long straight road ahead going up; another hill, who cares, I can handle them OK now. The adrenaline is flowing as we get closer so the hill is conquered with little or no difficulty even in the hot sun.

At the top, there is a monument to the most famous pilgrim of modern times, Pope John Paul II. He didn't have to walk, no he came in a plane and then a Pope mobile. We are only joking but we christen him the greatest Touregrino of them all. On the not so funny side, my foot is really sore now. Its aching like it is badly bruised. It should be OK tomorrow but if not I will pop a couple of pain killers to get me over the finish line. It is going to be strange on Friday morning when we don't have to get up and go walking again.

The albergue here is more like a military barracks. It was specially built I am told for the last Holy Year. That is the time when the feast of St James, the 25th July, falls on a Sunday. It will be on Saturday in 2015 when I hope to come back but as the following year is a leap year it skips the Sunday and falls on a Monday. I have no intention of trying to work out when the next Holy year will be but it will be long after my walking days are over. Well, I have worked it out, I will be 72 in 2021, the next Holy Year and if God spares me and I still have all my faculties, well, who knows. Never say never. And to think, I said I would never do it again but by the time I got this far in my narrative, I am thinking about another two pilgrimages. What is it about this thing that keeps calling us back.

There does not seem to be anywhere to get dinner in this little town. One resident tells us to turn to the left and we will find a place. He forgot to say it was the second turn left but eventually we found the restaurant. A classier looking place than we are used to. It is on the main road to Santiago and has its own car parking so you may guess, it is a fairly large place. The food was good and the wine was fine.

Before going back to the albergue and bed, we stop to look at the lights of Santiago below us. It is no wonder this place is known as 'the mount of joy', Monte del Gozo

Buenos Noches y Buen Camino

Monte del Gozo to Santiago

Day 27, Thursday, 3rd October

It's an early start again but we are stopped dead in our tracks when Mees gets a phone call from home telling him about a death. He tries to keep a brave face but I can see he is visibly shaken. To make matters worse, we are just a short distance down the road and it starts to rain quite heavy. It rained all night, so much so that you wonder where nature got any more from to chuck down on us. The lord is trying to let us know that we are not to be too proud today. It is a time to be humble.

We are in the outskirts now and we find a little bar to have our last Camino breakfast. Any more after this will be more at our leisure. Coffee and croissants as we watch a man empty the slot machines, how exciting, but when you think about it, it's the first sign of modern materialistic life we have seen for over a month.

The slog into town seems more than the actual distance but at least the rain has stopped. I am keeping my poncho on though just in case. Down a street where road works are going on so we have to dodge a JCB and then we hear the skirl of the

bagpipes. Under an arch just before the main square is a busker playing the pipes and a few beggars, round one final corner and there it is, the Cathedral of Santiago, Praza Obradoiro. This has been what we have been walking towards all this time, our goal, our final destination, the resting

[164]

place of Santiago, St Jacob, Saint James the greater, the apostle chosen by Jesus to walk with him and to share the same chalice. He was the first apostle to face and accept death for the love of Jesus. Of all the apostles only one was not martyred, James' brother John. He was entrusted with the care of Mary, who was probably his aunt. All the rest of them accepted death rather than renounce the risen Christ.

We have some time yet until the pilgrim mass at noon so we make our way to the pilgrim office to claim our compostelas. They accept that I started from Pamplona even though I went home and restarted from Burgos. I should have told them I started from St James Gate in Dublin, the traditional starting place for the Irish pilgrims; the gate was there long before Mr Arthur Guinness. On the way back, we stumble upon the Correos, (post office) so I go in to collect my parcel. At this moment God decides to throw some more bad weather at two overly proud pilgrims. There is a ferocious gust of wind and the skies open. It's not just rain, it's a mini gale. My parcel is saturated and starting to fall apart and believe it or not, after 800km walking, we are lost. Even Mees has lost his bearings and that's unusual for this old sailor. We are sheltering in the door of a bank so what the heck, I am going to ask directions which they are glad to give, could you see that happen in Belfast, I think not. At last we are back at the Catedral and can find our way to the only albergue within the old city limits, O Fogar de Teodomiro. It seems fine and we book for two nights but we will find out later why we should not recommend it to anyone else.

There is internet here but once again, I cannot get my boarding pass printed. The problem is that there is no Adobe reader to generate the printable pass, don't they use Adobe in Spain? I will just have to find the internet café and hope they have Adobe but for now, the Pilgrim Mass is our priority.

We make our way back to the Catedral to find lots of broken umbrellas lying about. The gale was sent not just for us I laugh.

The Cathedral is fairly full when we enter. All the seats are taken by tourists, many of whom are spreading themselves well out as if saving seats for others. Basically pews that can seat 5 are currently seating 4 or even just 3 with bags taking the other seats. Peregrinos are standing up the sides and down the back. The people who walked 800km to get here must stand, the

[165]

ones who came in on the morning cruise ship get seats, so much for it being the Pilgrim Mass.

A nun is leading us in singing but unfortunately, everything is in Spanish so it's hard to follow but she has a beautiful voice so it is enjoyable to listen to. The area just in front of the altar and under the Botafumeiro is cordoned off even though there are seats there but I don't know why. Anyhow, Mees and I find a good spot to stand at the back of one of the cross sections. Announcements are made to the effect that cameras should not be used during the mass and the guided tours should now stop. The statues took more notice. The tours continue and the cameras keep flashing but strangely, the security people or maybe I should call them stewards are hassling pilgrims about their backpacks. We had heard that backpacks were not allowed but the people in the pilgrim office said it was OK as it was our mass. The stewards are doing nothing about the tours or cameras. As the mass proceeds both tours and cameras die off but never cease.

I have noticed that some people are being admitted to the closed off section so assume they are VIPs of some sort but I really should be paying more attention to the mass. My mind wanders to the millions of pilgrims who have stood here before me over the centuries and it is quite humbling to think of the hardships they had to put up with to stand in this same spot and listen to the same mass; I feel quite small and humble actually. I feel in the presence of Jesus but also in the presence of St James and the souls of all those people, less able than I to make this pilgrimage, who are now in heaven. They say that making this pilgrimage is penance for all the sins of your past life and all is forgiven and from this day, the pilgrim starts off with a clean slate. The plenary indulgence gained by each pilgrim supposedly halves your time in Purgatory unless you make it in a Holy Year, then you get off purgatory completely. What it certainly does is make you think about your life and your place in God's plan. At last the mass gets to the communion and a priest comes up to the standing pilgrims so that they can receive the Eucharist without all going to the altar. As I wait in line, a tourist about four pews in front of us must think they are giving out souvenirs and pushes his way into the queue and as the priest holds up the host and says, in Spanish of course, 'The Body of Christ', this guy reaches out and snatches the host and makes off back to his seat. I can't be sure but I think he put it in his pocket. He definitely was not Catholic, no Catholic anywhere in this world would ever receive communion in such a disrespectful manner. By the way, the reverence shown by Mees is extremely respectful, in fact, he would put many Catholics to shame.

As the mass is coming to an end I notice the tiraboleiros preparing to light the botafumeiro. I thought this only happened on special occasions but hey, I am not complaining, it is a sight I did not expect to see. By the way, I did not know at the time that the attendants were called tiraboleiros, that is thanks to Mr Brierley whose guide for this part I read more closely when I got home. Also, and this I did know at the time, the reason for swinging the botafumeiro with the burning incense dates back to medieval times and was used to hide the smell of the many unwashed pilgrims.

Now, so much for no cameras. At this point one of the priests on the altar pulls up his robes and produces an iPhone from his pocket and starts to record the event. If it's good enough for him then it's good enough for me so out comes my camera and it is on to video. It is an amazing sight as the botafumeiro swings higher and higher and finishes its arc just above my head and then swings directly away from me. Once again, a small decision turned out to be a very good one, I could not have asked for a better spot to watch this happen. At last it comes to rest and the Pilgrim Mass is over. This has been almost a guiding light for us and it decided the timing we choose to enter the city. I can't help wonder if they swung the botafumeiro at the next day's mass or were we just lucky.

I am left pondering the whole camino now. A bit of a theme park type experience for tourists in the cathedral, a bit of a race from Sarria and why oh why do pilgrims feel the need to graffiti every monument and road sign they come to. The amount of scribbling on anything that stands still from Sarria onwards is just plain wrong in my opinion. I have never felt the need to write my name anywhere other than in guest books. But if only one person gets from it what I am getting, and will continue to get in the coming months, then it is all worthwhile.

Before leaving the Cathedral, I spotted a familiar face. It is Sean who I met way back in Castrojeriz. He is now with his wife who flew out to meet him at Sarria and walk the last section with him. She feels the need to apologise to me for not doing the whole thing but I reassure her that her pilgrimage is of just as much value as mine. Everybody has their own way, every pilgrimage is private and I hope every pilgrimage is as fulfilling as mine. I do believe that Mees has found his extremely fulfilling and I know his life will now take a turn for the better. No one deserves it more than him.

Beside the albergue is a little restaurant that specialises in good healthy well-presented food. We had planned to find a genuine tapas bar but this place really fits the bill for now but it does not do dinners so we must find somewhere to eat tonight. You would think this would be easy given that every little town and village catered well for the pilgrim. Not so easy in Santiago but we found an Italian pizza place and that was good enough for tonight. The pizza was great, the beer was grand as was the wine but after dinner the routine was different from usual. We no longer had to be in by 9pm so we wandered around town for a while and then back to the little restaurant beside the albergue for a nightcap

Buenos Noches y Buen Camino

A Day in Santiago

Day 28, Friday, 4th October

What a luxury this morning, lying late, well 9am which to us over the last month seems decadent to say the least. Round by the Cathedral, we found a little café for breakfast and then visited the cathedral again to take some more photos. This is followed by a shopping trip around the souvenir shops. Souvenirs range from a couple of Euros to hundreds but my only purchase is a lapel pin of the pilgrim shell, a snow globe for my daughter's collection and a fridge magnet for Margaret's collection. I am sure we went for lunch, but do you know, I have no recollection of it. This part of my story is being written from memory only as I did not keep a journal after we arrived in Santiago. I know we did go for a walk to find out where the stop was to get the bus to the bus station in the morning. From the station I will get the airport bus and Mees will get the bus to take him home to the Netherlands. I have learned to stop calling his country Holland which is only a province. It is like calling Ireland Leinster although I imagine the Dubs would not mind that. Mees has opted for a bus journey home which will take him around 32 hours, I will miss him but I do not envy him.

 As we walk back to the Cathedral, we see people we have met along the way like the guy who had a little trolley attached to a harness that he pulled along instead of a rucksack. Sitting on a wall enjoying the sunshine and writing her journal is Almut. I am really glad to see her again. She is feeling much better and the tendonitis is no longer a problem but she still will not be able to walk to Finisterre as she had planned, so she is taking a bus tomorrow as we go home.

The rest of the day is spent wandering around the city, taking photographs and then going for dinner. We finished again in the little restaurant beside the albergue.

We met a Danish guy here but I can't remember which night it was. Maybe it was last night but he had a lot of euros to get rid

[169]

of and was in for a drinking session. We all finished off kind of drunk. Definitely last night I think. Was I that drunk that I can't remember which night was which. Who cares, it was great craic but the more I reminisce I think it was last night.

What I do remember is the reason not to stay in this albergue at a weekend. Directly below our window is the albergue bar. In Spain, the Friday night revelry does not start until well after 22:00 but when it starts, it goes on till about 4am. However, even though the patrons have left the bar downstairs, the people who have left other bars further into town are still passing by right up to about 6am. It's a good job we are not walking tomorrow as we got no sleep at all tonight

Buenos Noches y Buen Camino

Santiago to Dublin and Belfast

Day 29, Saturday, 5th October. The Last Day

We need to be in the bus station before 10am as Mees has to catch his bus to the Netherlands. Since we have just walked El Camino, we decide that we will walk to the bus station so for the last time we put on our backpacks and start walking. It only takes 20 minutes to get there and we sit down for our last coffee together although bus station coffee is not very good. As we relax together for the last time, Almut arrives to catch her bus to Finisterre. Sadly the next bus to the airport is in 20 minutes so the moment I have been dreading is upon us. I must say goodbye to Mees for the last time. It is emotional. We have been in each other's pockets, as we say in Ireland, for the last 20 days and in that time he has become a closer friend than people I have known for 20 years.

The journey to the airport is a sad one and sitting in the terminal on my own staring out the window seems longer than the whole Camino. Now, on the plane, other passengers seem distant and not up to talking to strangers, the complete opposite to the flight out. The flight home seems like forever

but at last I arrive in Dublin to find Margaret, Christopher and Sarah waiting for me. Margaret is not impressed with my beard but Chris thinks it is great.

My camino is nearly over but it will not finish until I touch that Camino waymark tile on my own front door.

It's finished. I am home but part of me will forever be in northern Spain. In Navarre, the Basque country, La Rioja, Leon and Castille, Galicia and Santiago, on the top of Mont Perdón, La Cruz de Ferro, Montes de Leon and of course O Cebreiro. Another little bit of me will travel to the Netherlands with Mees.

I had said all along that I would never return and could not understand people going back time and again but now that I am home I know that I must return. I still don't understand it but the Camino is calling me back and back I shall go if God spares me for another few years, after all, I have to find all those little bits of my heart that I left behind

For the last time

Buenos Noches y Buen Camino

Epilogue

I still do not fully understand why peregrinos go back year after year but the Camino undoubtedly calls you back. Two things have prevented me returning this year. Three weeks after I came home in October, my wife had a stroke and I don't feel ready to leave her just yet. The other problem is time. I don't want to walk during the heat of summer and spring and autumn are not feasible this year but as it is, I plan to return around the middle of April 2015 and this time start in St Jean Pied de Port. I am praying for a mild winter and warm spring in the Pyrenees so that I can walk the Route Napoleon. I had hoped that my friend Mees could return with me but I heard recently that the Camino, in his case, does provide. Without revealing any confidences, his life has taken a great turn for the better but it means that for next year at least, he is too busy to return. All the candles and prayers for him in Santiago have come up trumps.

To all young people, the best advice I can give you is, 'do it now'. Don't wait until you are my age as you will need the years to go back time and again.

As the days pass, I find myself reflecting more and more on the feelings I experienced each day on pilgrimage and I see so much of what I learnt in everyday life. I always believed that God was to be found in nature and the Camino has reinforced this. The budding of new life each spring and the trees dropping their leaves in autumn so as to withstand the winter storms convinces me that this world was not created by random occurrences. The beauty of this world is God's masterpiece and the crossing of Spain on the Camino shows us every facet of it. To quote John Muir again, *"going to the mountains is going home"*. He said the same for forests. It is so true. Although it was at times tough going, I have never felt more at home than I did in Spain or more free than, having literally exhausted my body, stood at the top of a mountain and looked back at the vista below. I found Jesus in every field, vineyard, forest trail and mountain goat path up and down the mountains. I learnt how to talk to him and call him 'buddy'.

Maybe I do understand why peregrinos go back time and again whereas those just there for the walk move onto something else. We want to experience that feeling of peace, freedom and being completely at home again and again.

[173]

I found this quote in a little CTS publication, Santiago de Compostela, sometime after arriving home. I think it says what I was feeling along the way and particularly at the pilgrim mass.

I felt the fatigue, hunger and pain of those hundreds of thousands who have gone before

I felt their presence. I also shared their joy, awe and elation

I'll be back

Photographs

Mont Perdón

Poco Poco Los Arcos

The Friendly Dog

San Juan de Acre ruins

Carrión de los Condes

La Virgen Del Camino

Hospital de Orbigo

**Graffiti on Galician Boundary
Marker**

The Botafumeiro

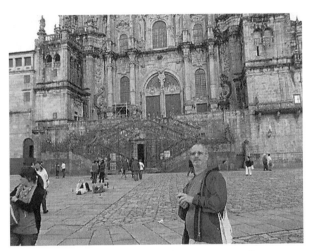

Mees in Santiago de Compostela

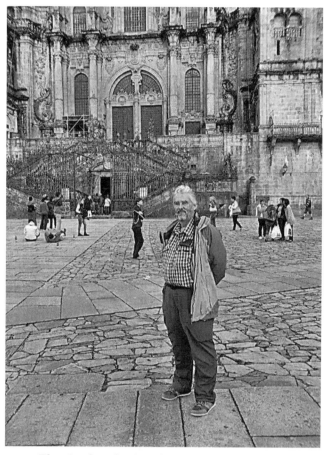

The Author in Santiago de Compostela

Bibliography

The New Testament

John Brierley - A Pilgrims Guide to the Camino de Santiago

Hape Kerkeling - I'm Off Then

David Baldwin - Santiago de Compostela, The Pilgrim Way of St James

Bill Walker - The Best Way

Robert Hamilton - Camino de Santiago, Walking the Camino Francés

Mary Platt Parmele - A Short History of Spain

Eyewitness Travel - Back Roads Spain

Web Pages of

>   The Irish Confraternity at www.stjamesirl.com

>   The British Confraternity at www.csj.org.uk including the address by Laurie Dennett

>   www.newadvent.org

>   Gonzalo Lopez at www.via-compostela.com

>   And the help given to me for my pilgrimage by the many great people on the forum, www.caminodesantiago.me

Via Google

>   La Chanson de Roland

>   Quotes of John Muir and writings of Eusebius

Photographs not my own,

Page 1, 24, 54, 43, 175 & 176 courtesy of Christopher McHugh

Page 133   courtesy of Mees Van Der Sluijs

8275782R00106

Printed in Great Britain
by Amazon.co.uk, Ltd.,
Marston Gate.